"To travel hopefully is a better thing than to arrive, and the true success is to labor." —Robt Louis Stevenson

PHILOSOPHICAL IMAGINATION

and the Evolution of Modern Philosophy

"There will be time to audit the accts later, There will be sunlight later, And the equation will come out at last." — Louis MacNeice —

"The world is round so that friendship may encircle it." — Pierre Teilhard de Chardin

"And speech impelled us to... urge the mind to After sight + foresight." —T.S. Eliot—

PHILOSOPHICAL IMAGINATION

and the

Evolution of Modern Philosophy

> "Th'k'g is to me the greatest fatigue in the wrld."
>
> "Skepticism is the chastity of the intellect, and it is shameful to surrender it too soon or to the 1st comer."
> — Geo. Santayana

James P. Danaher

PARAGON HOUSE

First Edition 2017

Published in the United States by
Paragon House
Saint Paul, Minnesota

www.ParagonHouse.com

Copyright © 2017 by Paragon House

All rights reserved. No part of this book may be reproduced, in any form, without written permission from the publisher, unless by a reviewer who wishes to quote brief passages.

Bible references from the New Revised Standard Version unless otherwise noted.

Library of Congress Cataloging-in-Publication Data

    Names: Danaher, James P., author.
    Title: Philosophical imagination and the evolution of modern philosophy / by James P. Danaher.
    Description: First edition. | Saint Paul, Minnesota : Paragon House, 2017.
    Identifiers: LCCN 2017010532 | ISBN 9781557789303 (pbk. : alk. paper)
    Subjects: LCSH: Philosophy, Modern--History.
    Classification: LCC B791 .D36 2017 | DDC 190--dc23 LC record available at https://lccn.loc.gov/2017010532

    Manufactured in the United States of America
    10 9 8 7 6 5 4 3 2 1

The paper used in this publication meets the minimum requirements of American National Standard for Information Sciences—Permanence of Paper for Printed Library Materials, ANSIZ39.48-1984.

For my former and present students

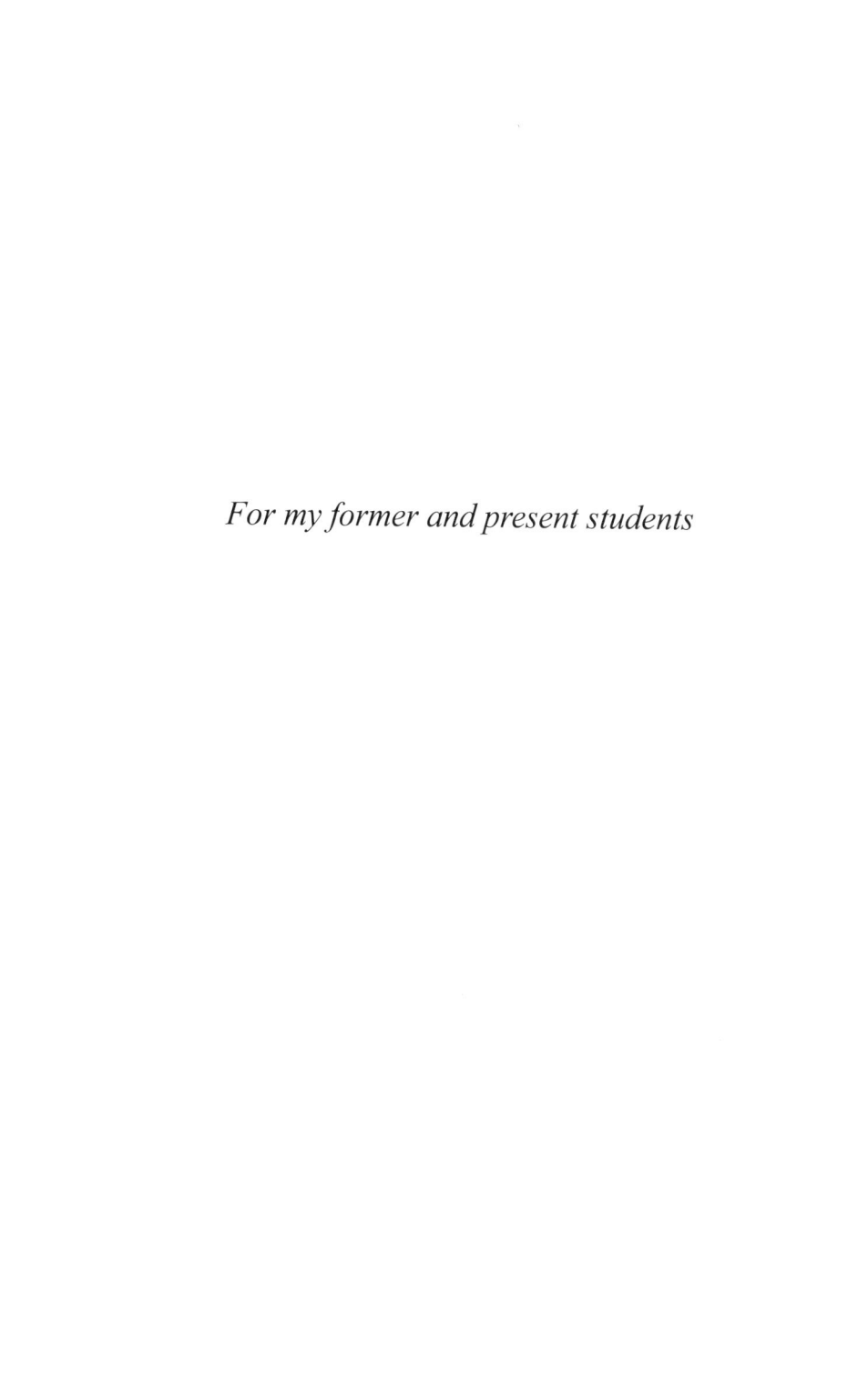

Acknowledgment

I would like to acknowledge my indebtedness to Willard K. Pottinger, whose faithful friendship, proofreading, editing, and encouragement has contributed greatly to several of my books.

Contents

Introduction ix

CHAPTER ONE
The Ancient and Medieval World: Plato and Aristotle 1

CHAPTER TWO
Advent of the Modern Mind: Corpuscular Philosophy 19

CHAPTER THREE
Immaterialists: Gottfried Wilhelm Leibniz and George Berkeley. . .33

CHAPTER FOUR
The Kinds Problem: Rene Descartes and John Locke. 49

CHAPTER FIVE
A Priori and A Posteriori: David Hume and Immanuel Kant 63

CHAPTER SIX
Historicism: Immanuel Kant and G. W. F. Hegel 77

CHAPTER SEVEN
Existentialism: Albert Camus and Soren Kierkegaard. 93

CHAPTER EIGHT
Pragmatism: William James 107

CHAPTER NINE
Authenticity and Hermeneutics: Martin Heidegger and
   Hans Georg Gadamer 121

CHAPTER TEN
The Linguistic Turn: Saussure, Wittgenstein, and Third Wave
   Feminism. 137

CHAPTER ELEVEN
The End of the Metanarrative: Thomas Kuhn and
   Jean-Francois Lyotard 153

CHAPTER TWELVE
Philosophy and Theology in the Twenty-first Century: Toward a
   Broader Concept of Truth 161

Introduction

When someone mentions philosophy, what comes to mind? Do you think of logic and rational arguments? Maybe the mention of philosophy brings to mind abstract questions that most people suppose have little to do with the actual affairs of life. Whatever your initial concept of philosophy happens to be, however, the contention of this book is that philosophy is most essentially a form of thinking or kind of intelligence. It is certainly the least understood form of intelligence, perhaps because it is so radically different from other forms of intelligence.

Intelligence on its most basic level is about acquiring and retaining information. We hear parents brag about how brilliant their toddlers are because of how quickly and accurately they absorb information. This is certainly our earliest form of intelligence but there is nothing critical about it. Small children record information indiscriminately from whatever sources are available. Critical thinking can begin only after we have acquired enough information to form an understanding, which then enables us to evaluate future information to see if it conforms to that understanding. Some philosophical thinking does take place on this level, as when we test arguments for validity or examine the internal coherence of certain philosophical positions. Philosophy, however, as a unique form of intelligence is quite different. In fact, philosophical thinking is the inverse of critical thinking, in that instead of using our understanding to evaluate data, it allows

ix

certain data to destroy portions of our understanding that the philosophical imagination might create a new conceptual understanding that can make sense of the data that our previous understanding could not.

How this happens is mysterious. Although most of us have some experience of making minor adjustments to our understanding because of new data, when we do, we most often simply acquire that new perspective from someone else, but what about the one who originally came up with that new understanding or perspective? What kind of thinking or intelligence produces a new way to see what is before us? This is what we are really after in studying philosophy. To that end, we will examine those individuals throughout the history of philosophy who excelled at this form of thinking that we might gain insight into its unique nature and therein develop something of a philosophical intelligence for ourselves.

Thus, instead of simply explaining the different schools of philosophy (e.g., modern materialism, immaterialism, rationalism, empiricism, phenomenalism, historicism, existentialism, pragmatism, hermeneutics, linguistic philosophy, and feminism), we will consider the circumstances and events that forced the philosophical imaginations of certain individuals to develop these new ways to conceptualize our experience. By understanding philosophy in the context of such a narrative, we not only come to better understand this unique form of intelligence and the perspectives it has created, but equally we gain insight into the evolution of human consciousness which has created the modern minds we inherit. An understanding of this evolving modern mind allows us to see our world and our human condition within it from a twenty-first century perspective. Without such a perspective, we view the world and our human condition through antiquated lenses that only allow us to see a world gone by and not the world that is unfolding before us.

Of course, the world does not change but our understanding of it certainly does, and it changes because new data present anomalies to our inherited perspectives. When we face data that defy our inherited perspectives, we either must deny the threatening data or become philosophical and re-conceptualize our understanding in order to accommodate it. In other words, either we can pretend that our way of conceptualizing our experience somehow represents ultimate reality and thus reject the upsetting data, or we exercise our philosophical imagination in order to pursue a perspective that better accounts for what is before us.

Map of the Story

The Ancient World

Heraclitus	Parmenides	Plato	Aristotle
535-475 BCE	515-460 BCE	c 428-348 BCE	c. 384-322 BCE

The Christian Medieval World

Augustine	Christian	Thomas Aquinas	Scholastic
354-430 AD	Platonism	1225-1274 AD	Aristotelianism

The Modern World

Corpuscular Philosophy and the End of Aristotle

The Immaterialists

Gottfried Wilhelm Leibniz 1646-1716   George Berkeley 1685-1753

Modern Rationalism	*Modern Empiricism*	*Phenomenalism*
Rene Descartes	John Locke	Immanuel Kant
1596-1650	1632-1704	1724-1804
	David Hume	
	1711-1776	

Historicism	*Pragmatism*	*Existentialism*
G.W.F. Hegel	William James	Soren Kierkegaard
1770-1831	1842-1910	1813-1855

The Linguistic Turn	*Hermeneutics*	*Feminism*
Ferdinand de Saussure	Martin Heidegger	2000
1857-1913	1889-1976	
Ludwig Wittgenstein	Hans Georg Gadamer	
1889-1951	1900-2002	

The End of the Metanarrative

Thomas Kuhn	Jean-Francois Lyotard
1922-1996	1924-1998

CHAPTER ONE

The Ancient and Medieval World: Plato and Aristotle

Philosophy as a form of thinking or kind of intelligence most likely had its origins long before we began to record history. Historically, however, we mark its beginnings with a group of Greek philosophers who came to be known as Pre-Socratics since they preceded Socrates (470/469–399 BCE). These Pre-Socratic philosophers were from different parts of the Greek world, which extended from what is today Greece to western Turkey in the east and to southern Italy and Sicily in the west. Perhaps because they were from different parts of the Greek world, they represented a variety of views about the world and our lives within it. In light of these different views, it seemed obvious, at least to some, that human experience was not simply a matter of recording data but that we had a certain freedom concerning how to organize and understand that data. Thus, it seemed that in addition to whatever sensory apparatus and mental hardware we all shared, we also possessed an imagination, which allows us to conceptualize and think about the world in different ways.

Many people find this terrifying since a great deal of security comes from thinking that we do not have freedom in this regard and the world is as we have learned to perceive it. Many simply accept the perspective they inherit from their culture and language community and find security in equating that perspective with truth itself. When such people encounter others who think differently, they often see them as enemies, since that different perspective threatens what they imagine to be truth. There are others, however, whose encounter with different perspectives stimulates their philosophical imagination. This was certainly the case with Socrates.

By the time of Socrates, many visiting professors, known as sophists, had visited Athens, and exposed the population to a host of different perspectives. The basic subject matter these sophists taught was rhetoric or speechmaking, and many of Athens' youth found the idea of learning to make intelligent sounding speeches something worthwhile to acquire. The Athenian establishment, however, was not happy with some of the unsettling alternative perspectives that these foreigners offered along with teaching the art of oratory. Socrates, although not a foreigner or sophist, was perhaps the most unsettling of all, since he found problems with not only the numerous sophists who visited Athens, but with the Athenian establishment as well, which eventually led to his execution at the hands of the state.

Socrates never wrote a book or developed a philosophy. His student, Plato (c. 428/427 or 424/423–348/347 BCE), however, wrote over thirty dialogues in which Socrates appears as the primary interlocutor in all but the late dialogues, which Plato wrote toward the end of his life. In those dialogues, Socrates is still present but plays a diminished role. It is hard to know how closely the literary character, Socrates, resembles the historical character. The one dialogue that does accurately depict the historical Socrates is

The Apology, which is the account of Socrates' trial. We know it to be historically accurate since Xenophon (c. 430–354 BCE) also writes of the same historical event and confirms Plato's account. The rest of what we know about Socrates comes through the genius of Plato, thus making it hard to distinguish the historical Socrates from the literary character. Apart from *The Apology*, perhaps there is something of the historical Socrates represented in the early dialogues that center on his life and death, but with the rest of the dialogues most believe that the Socrates that appears there is more a literary character of Plato's creation.

Plato provides a great example from which to begin our story about the philosophical imagination, since it is easy to see what stimulated his thinking. As is generally the case, the philosophical imagination arises out of a conflict. We can trace the conflict that was particularly pertinent to Plato's philosophical perspective to the pre-Socratic philosophers, Heraclitus (535–475 BCE) and Parmenides (c. 515–c. 465 BCE). The conflict centered on the difference between the way we experience the world and the way we think about it.

Heraclitus was from what is today western Turkey, and Parmenides from today's southern Italy. Heraclitus based his thinking upon observation or experience in the ordinary sense. This began an empiricist tradition in philosophy. The problem with empiricism down to our present day is that it is never certain and always leads to some form of skepticism. Heraclitus' skepticism resulted from the fact that the world as we experience it is in constant flux. Things constantly change and therefore result in contradictions: warm things grow cold, cold things grow warm, damp things become dry, and dry things become damp. Heraclitus thought this made any fixed and certain knowledge of the world impossible.

Unlike Heraclitus, Parmenides believed that knowledge in the form of certainty was possible, but it did not originate by considering the things we know with our senses. Parmenides was of the Pythagorean school of thought that believed that only what was ultimately real was knowable. For Parmenides, things that were ultimately real were immutable and eternal. Of course, nothing we experience with our senses is immutable and eternal; so Parmenides, and the rationalist tradition that would follow, pointed to mathematics and geometry as examples of the type of thinking that would lead to knowledge. Unlike the things we experience with our senses, which are in constant flux, the three angles of any triangle always equal 180 degrees, and circles are always figures whose every point is equidistant from the center. The kinds of things we think about in mathematics and geometry are very different from the ever-changing world of experience. We can be certain of numbers and geometrical concepts because they are not constantly becoming something other than themselves. This way of thinking maintained that such immutable and eternal objects represented *being* rather than the constant *becoming* that we experience in the world of our senses. Thus, Parmenides made a distinction between *being*, which was knowable because it was immutable and eternal, and *becoming*, which was not knowable because it was in constant flux. Parmenides thought that knowledge had to focus on *being* rather than *becoming*. Consequently, such a focus would lead us into abstract thinking and away from the world of actual experience.

At the base of these two different perspectives lay the question of what constituted ultimate reality. Is reality the world that we experience with our empirical senses, of which we can never be certain, or is it the abstract world of our clear and distinct ideas, which have little to do with our actual experience but seem more real in the sense of being immutable and eternal? It would not be until the latter part of the twentieth century that we would gain insight into the connection between these two very different ways of thinking and the two very different hemispheres of the human brain. The Greeks knew of the bicameral nature of the human brain, but we came to know the way these two hemispheres specialize in different ways of thinking only with the invention of the MRI. Although both hemispheres work together and it is not quite as simple as one hemisphere specializing in one form of thinking and the other in another, there are two very different logics that dominant the two hemispheres of the brain. Ultimately, the difference between Heraclitus and Parmenides may have been more a matter of one man being dominantly right-brained, while the other was more left-brained. However without the insight that the MRI has provided us today, Plato had to come up with a very different understanding if he wanted to claim that both men had valuable insights. His basic leaning was more toward Parmenides, and he believed that ideas that were immutable and eternal represented a greater reality than the reality we encounter with our empirical experience but he wanted to grant the world of experience a higher status than mere illusion.

In order to understand Plato's solution, we should note that one main point that Plato and Socrates seemed to share was an interest in the idea of the *good life*. Like many Athenian Greeks, they both believed that one could achieve the good life only by acquiring certain virtues. The four cardinal Greek virtues were courage, temperance, wisdom, and justice. Almost all of the dialogues focus on these and other virtues. For Plato, knowledge of these virtues was the key to acquiring them for oneself, but it was not a practical knowledge of such things, which simply allowed us to perform such virtues. What the dialogues are after is a perfect knowledge that would give us an understanding of the virtues that resemble the kind of knowledge we have in mathematics and geometry. Plato thought that if we had an understanding of courage or justice as precise as our understanding of a circle, as a figure whose every point is equidistant from the center, or the number seven which is always the same and universally recognized, we could teach virtue as precisely as we teach geometry and mathematics. We have a sufficient knowledge of geometry and mathematics because we know exactly what a circle is and what the numeral seven is. We know such things through the intellect alone, apart from sense experience. Sense experience, however, gives us a variety of different instances labelled *courage*, *justice*, or *love*, thus, leaving us with confused notions of such things, especially when we compare our concepts of them with our concept of a *circle* or *seven*. Because of this, the dialogues are constantly trying to get beyond the instances of virtues in order to know their pure form. Plato thought that the instances or examples that we point to as courage, justice, or love were just bad representations of such things, just as any circle we draw is a bad representation and is never a figure whose every point is exactly equidistant from the center. Plato always has the character Socrates trying to get at the pure form of such virtues by trying to know them through the intellect alone, the way we know geometry or mathematics.

Plato employs different strategies in trying to get at these pure forms. One strategy was to have Socrates question his interlocutors in order to get at the immutable and eternal essence of a concept by trying to see what is common in all of the instances of something like courage or justice. All sevens are the same and, because of that, we have a perfect knowledge of mathematics. Thus, Socrates is always trying to understand the virtues the same way we know mathematics, that is, by discovering the essence or the single characteristic that is always present in all instances of a particular virtue. Likewise, if we wanted to get at the immutable and eternal form of virtue itself we would try to abstract the common denominator or essence that runs through all the virtues; that is, what do the virtues all have in common?

Plato uses a variety of devices to try to get us thinking on this higher, abstract level of the immutable and eternal forms. Perhaps his most famous device appears in the seventh book of Plato's *Republic* where Socrates explains the Platonic project to the interlocutor, Glaucon, through what we have come to know as the *allegory of the cave*. The story he tells is of people held captive since their youth in a cave. Their chains prevent them from turning their heads and they can see only the back wall of the cave that is in front of them. Behind them are both a fire that sheds light on the back wall of the cave and a parapet atop which men parade holding a variety of objects. The light from the fire, combined with the objects the puppeteers hold up above the parapet create shadows on the back wall of the cave. The prisoners see the shadows, but since they never see anything but shadows, they imagine them not to be shadows at all but as much reality as exists. In fact, if they were ever able to turn their head and look into the brightness of the fire or, worse, if they were dragged out into the sunlight, they would be blinded by the light and seek to retreat into the shadowy reality of the cave where they were able to see. Furthermore, if someone tried to tell them that the shadows, which they were able to see, were not as real as the things that exist in the light that blinded them, they would find that unreasonable and difficult to believe. If, however, someone ventured into the sunlight and allowed his eyes to adjust to the light, he would see the greater reality outside of the cave. Now if that same individual were to return to his place in the cave, he would find it difficult to treat the shadows as real. Likewise, he would find it equally difficult to convince his fellow cave dwellers that he had encountered a greater reality that revealed the shadows of the cave to be less real than the cave dwellers imagined. Socrates then goes on to explain that the ascent out of the cave is the ascent of the soul into the intellectual world where one would encounter the true form of things rather than merely their shadows. In the allegory, Plato points toward two very different experiences: one of a shadowy world whose sensory objects flash in and out of existence and the other of the clear and distinct experience of things perceived by the intellect alone. His hope was that philosophy might provide us with the means to ascend to that higher level of reality and knowledge.

In the eighth book of *Republic*, Plato presents another way of explaining the different levels of reality and our knowledge of those levels. Philosophers refer to this section as *the simile of the line*. There, Socrates explains several levels of reality as well as the kinds of knowledge by which we know things on those levels. In addition to Heraclitus's level of reality that we experience with our senses, and Socrates represents with the shadows on the back wall of the cave, there is a lower level of reality. This lower level of reality is that of art or things that replicate physical reality. If physical reality is no more than the shadows on the back of the cave wall, then art is the shadow of those shadows. Such a realm is not as real as the physical world but it does possess some reality. In the late dialogues, Plato introduces an even lower level of reality. This lowest level of reality is that of lies or falsehoods, which must have some sort of reality because if lies and falsehoods do not exist, all statements must be true.

Moving up the line from physical reality, Plato sees mathematics and geometry dealing with a higher level of knowledge because its objects are immutable and eternal and therefore represent a greater level of reality than the objects of sense perception, which are neither immutable nor eternal. Above that level of realty, and likewise knowledge, are the immutable and eternal forms of things like courage, wisdom, justice, and love. Corresponding to each different level of reality, Plato thought different forms of knowledge would be required. Sensory knowledge is the way we know the world of empirical experience, while mathematics is the type of knowledge by which we know numbers and geometry. Plato's hope was that philosophy would be the form of knowledge by which we could know the ultimate form of things like wisdom, courage, and justice.

In what we consider the early and middle dialogues, Plato's notion of philosophy involves Socrates in rigorous dialogues with numerous interlocutors on various topics. The strategy in most of these is to have a particular interlocutor put forth his notions of what things like courage, love, justice, piety, or virtue are. Socrates then refutes an aspect of the notion so that the interlocutor might correct his thesis to account for the antithesis that Socrates presents. Of course, Socrates meets the interlocutor's new, refined thesis or synthesis with yet another objection or antithesis. The hope was that as Socrates refutes these earlier theses and forces the interlocutors to refine their concepts, they would finally arrive at the ultimate form that would need no further qualification. Unfortunately, although the dialogues do succeed at getting us a little clearer picture of the matter in question, they almost never get to the immutable and eternal form of such things. Most of the dialogues are aporetic; that is, they end in an impasse. Some twentieth century Plato scholars have argued that Plato never really had a philosophy but the intention of his work was simply to teach us how to think, or more precisely, how to develop a philosophical imagination that is able to think anew about what is before us.

Aristotle

Plato's student was Aristotle, who many think was the greatest of all philosophers. Aristotle was not an Athenian Greek, as were Socrates and Plato, but was born in Macedonia. Aristotle's father was the physician to Philip, king of Macedonia, and later in life Aristotle would become the tutor of Philip's son, Alexander the Great. At the age of eighteen, Aristotle's father sent his son to Athens to study at Plato's Garden Academy. That academy represented what many consider the first actual school in the West. Aristotle studied there with Plato for 20 years and only ceased his studies with Plato at the age of thirty-eight because Plato died. One might assume that if someone studied for twenty years under a philosopher as great as Plato, his thinking would look very much like his teacher's thinking. That was certainly not the case with Aristotle, nor is it generally the case with philosophy, since what the best philosophers teach is the philosophical imagination, which enables their students to conceptualize the world in better ways. Scholars build upon the knowledge of other scholars in order to advance our understanding of the world, but philosophers, especially philosophers as great as Aristotle, come up with entirely new ways to conceptualize the world.

Plato was certainly a good teacher of this philosophical imagination, and Aristotle was a superb student, but while Socrates and Plato focused predominantly on ethics and the idea of establishing the good life through knowledge of the virtues, Aristotle would move in a very different direction. Part of the reason for this was that Plato's theory of the forms was in trouble. In the dialogue, *Parmenides,* Plato attacks his own theory and shows its shortcomings. In the late dialogues toward the end of Plato's life, he attempts to shore up the theory but with little success. Thus, it is not surprising that Aristotle went in a different direction. That direction was toward the world we experience with our senses, and which Heraclitus thought was unknowable because everything we experience with our senses is constantly changing. In attempting to explain the world of our actual experience rather than the world of immutable and eternal forms, Aristotle, like Plato, maintained that things exist in different ways. Unlike Plato, however, who used the cave allegory or simile of the line to explain such different levels of existence, Aristotle looked to language.

By considering the nature of language, Aristotle saw that things were more complicated than either Heraclitus (becoming) or Parmenides (being) had imagined. What language revealed to Aristotle was that being was multifarious. To say that *blue* or *seven* exists is to talk about existence in two very different ways. Blue exists as a quality, while seven as a quantity. Likewise, *Athens* designates a place or position, while *cousin* designates a relation. Of these different categories of being, Aristotle thought that substances (like horses or trees) were different from other categories and were most real because substances were independent of all else in a way that other categories of being were not. Blue, seven, Athens, or cousin do not have being in the same way that a horse or tree has being. Blue or seven were descriptions of some substance's qualities or quantities, and Athens or cousins were either a place or relationship and had identity only in relationship to other things, while a tree was independent of all else and therefore most real, according to Aristotle. Thus, unlike Plato who thought the otherworldly forms were most real and independent of all else because they were eternal and immutable, Aristotle argued that substance was most real because it was central to language. Qualities, quantities, and relations are all about modifying substances. Aristotle says that a substance has "whatness" in a way that other things do not. When we speak of a quality like "blue", we must ask, what is blue, or if we speak of a quantity like "seven", again we must ask, seven what? Likewise, a relation like cousin points to a relation between substances. With language, everything seems to point toward substances, which Aristotle took to mean that substances were more real than other forms of existence like qualities, quantities, and relations. Interestingly, this idea that substance or that which is independent of all else is most real would eventually have an enormous effect upon Western thinking. In Eastern thought relation is often privileged over substance, and our connection to everything else is more important than being independent from all else. Most people living in the West, however, have inherited Aristotle's perspective of seeing substance as most real.

In building his philosophical perspective around the idea of substance, Aristotle argued that a substance had two components: form and matter—form being the thing that a substance shared with other members of its species, and matter being the thing that differentiated one member of a species from other members of that species. Consequently, a human being is not only the same as the person sitting next to him because they both have the same human form, but they are different from that other person because of their varying degrees of matter. These distinctions also explain why we have a greater knowledge of mathematics than of physics because numbers are purely formal and contain no matter. All sevens are the same seven and there is no matter which would individuate one seven from another. Mathematical concepts like seven or odd and even are immutable and eternal concepts, since they neither possess matter nor do they change over time, as living things do. Aristotle thought that these factors made mathematics a poor model for understanding nature. He believed that we could study nature but it would have to be an empirical rather than a rational study after the model of mathematics.

What made Aristotle's study of nature possible was his belief that language mirrored nature. Unlike Plato, who believed that the forms existed in another world, Aristotle believed the forms existed within substances themselves and our minds had the natural ability to identify those forms. While Plato had wanted to know the exact forms of moral kinds after the model of mathematics. Aristotle was not looking for exact definitions but simply an explanation for how we were able to group individual things into kinds or species. His explanation was that we possessed not only a passive intellect that simply recorded data through our empirical senses, but we also possessed an active intellect that actively detected the actual forms within things, to which we were then able to attach words that represented the actual kinds of things that existed within nature.

Another major part of Aristotle's philosophy concerned the idea of change. Plato had taken seriously Heraclitus' skepticism concerning the physical world because things were constantly changing and therefore unknowable in comparison to the immutable and eternal things we encounter in mathematics and geometry. Aristotle argued that the things we encounter with our senses are knowable but in a different way than mathematics was knowable. One of Aristotle's most famous dictums is that it is "the mark of an educated man to look for precision in each class of things just so far as the nature of the subject admits."

For Aristotle, we can know things in the physical world even though they change, because they change in patterned ways. Unlike the shadows on the back of a cave wall that flash in and out of existence, things within the physical world change slowly and according to a thing's specific nature. This was especially true of living things. What Aristotle observed was that living things changed and moved toward specific ends or purposes. So an acorn becomes an oak tree and a pinecone becomes a pine tree because within each is an end or *telos* toward which such living things are drawn. The fact that acorns always become oak trees and never

The Ancient and Medieval World: Plato and Aristotle 15

any other kind of thing, Aristotle took to mean that something must direct their growth toward that end and no other. He imagined that the end or *telos* of a thing must precede the growth of that thing and determine its changes. Thus, the *telos* or end, which is the chicken, must already exist within the egg in order to determine its changing from egg to chicken. In other words, the chicken must already be present as a potential within the egg in order for it to move toward that end. If this were not the case, some eggs would become chickens and some would become oak trees or any other kind of thing.

A little boy once asked if he would ever be as big as his father. When told that he would be as big or perhaps even bigger, the child asked, "Then where's the rest of me now?" Aristotle's answer is that it is there now but in potential rather than actuality; that is, things can exist both as actuality and potential and living things move from their potential to their actuality. Although the potential precedes the actuality in time, in other ways the actuality must precede the potential. Aristotle thought that since the actual is what gives meaning to the idea of potential, the actual must be present prior to the potential in order for a thing to change from potential to actual. The oak tree must already exist within the acorn at least as a *telos* or end that draws the acorn toward itself. Aristotle's explanation of the natural world caused later generations to consider him the first scientist, but his work went largely unnoticed in the West until the thirteenth century.

The Advent of Christianity

With the advent and spread of Christianity, there was need for a philosophical perspective that made sense and provided meaning for the beliefs and experiences of these early Christians. Although there were many philosophical influences that contributed to the early Christian perspective, the most notable of the early Christian philosophers was Augustine of Hippo (354–430 CE). After his conversion to Christianity, which he documents in his famous work, *The Confessions*, Augustine found much in Plato to be compatible with his new faith. Prior to his conversion to Christianity, several philosophical perspectives influenced Augustine's thinking in addition to that of Plato. After his conversion, however, Platonism had a more dominant influence. The aspect of Plato that was especially key to Augustine's Christian thinking was the Platonic idea that the things of this world were of the kinds or species they were because of their resemblance to the eternal and immutable forms that Plato thought existed in some other world. Augustine would argue that the Platonic forms did not exist in another world per se but rather existed as archetypal ideas within the mind of God. Thus, the things of this world are of the kind they are because of their resemblance to the archetypal ideas within God's mind. The book of Genesis in the Bible explains that God created the animals "after their kind";[1] but how could their kind exist before their creation unless their kind existed as an archetypal idea within the mind of God?

Augustine saw a strong connection between the otherworldliness of Plato and the other-worldliness of Christianity. In his monumental work, *The City of God* Augustine even speculates that perhaps Plato on one of his trips to Egypt passed through Palestine and actually met the prophet Jeremiah, and that Jeremiah had given

---

1. Gen. 1:25.

Plato the idea of another world. He dismissed the idea because Jeremiah's dates do not match up with the dates of Plato's trips to Egypt, but Augustine's ties to Plato and Neoplatonism had an enormous influence in shaping the first thousand years of Christianity.

The other factor that gave Plato such a central place in Augustinian thinking, and consequently much of the thinking of the early church, was the early Christian belief in the imminent return of Christ. If Christ was returning to usher in a new world and introduce something closer to the ideal realm of which Plato spoke, there was not much point in putting a lot of interest in the things of this world. Thus, the Platonic thinking of Augustine dominated early Christian thought. Although Aristotle was a late comer to the Western medieval world, when he came, his impact was enormous.

The story behind Aristotle's late arrival in the West begins with the fact that, unlike Plato whose works were available throughout the medieval world, Aristotle's formal writings did not survive the ancient world. What did survive were his lecture notes, but even those were largely unknown in the West and only preserved in the East by Muslim scholars. Aristotle's arrival in Western Europe came through the Moors in Spain. Muslim scholars at the University of Toledo translated Aristotle and other ancient texts into Latin during the twelfth and thirteenth centuries. Those manuscripts found their way to several European universities. At first, the church condemned the teachings of Aristotle, but Thomas Aquinas (1225–1274) eventually came up with an interpretation of Aristotle that the church found compatible with Christian teaching. With Thomas' canonization in 1323, Aristotle was well on his way to a place of dominance in late medieval thought. For the next four hundred years, the teachings of Aristotle had an enormous influence in molding Western thinking. The curriculum at most European universities well into the seventeenth century focused almost exclusively on Aristotle, and he became known, simply, as *The Philosopher*.

The Aristotelian thinking of Thomas Aquinas provided the church a systematic theology that certainly dominated the late medieval world, but this period also saw the occasional mystic. The medieval mystic tradition provided a very different way to see the world than the view provided by Aristotelian philosophy. As the name implies, the mystic tradition centered on the mystery that Aristotle and so many other philosophers had tried to eliminate or at least diminish. For the mystics, the mystery was not something to be solved but something to be experienced. It was a beholding often without analysis, or a beholding that defied analysis. Most mystics contended that genuine experiences of the Divine were beyond and very different from the way we experience other things. The wisdom that comes from such experiences is apophatic rather than kataphatic, that is, wisdom that comes from not knowing or the recognition that some of our experiences would forever exceed our understanding.

The seventeenth century, however, brought the seeds of what would eventually undermine Aristotle and the mystics alike. The exploration of the new world brought back tales of a world no one had ever imagined. Furthermore, the end of the 16th century saw the invention of the microscope and the beginning of the 17th century saw the invention of the telescope. Suddenly, the world was very different from what both Aristotle and the mystics had imagined, and a new way of seeing the world was on the horizon.

CHAPTER TWO

Advent of the Modern Mind: Corpuscular Philosophy

The sixteenth and seventeenth centuries revealed worlds previously unknown. The discovery of remote cultures provided an enormous amount of anthropological data, and the telescope gave access to more celestial data that provided support for Copernicus' speculation concerning a heliocentric rather than geocentric universe. The big event, however, that would eventually mark the end of Aristotle, as the dominant influence over Western thought, was the invention of the microscope and the world that it revealed.

Without the microscope, Aristotle and Thomas Aquinas could only imagine a way to conceptualize the world of their experience. From that limited experience, they had made a distinction between primary and secondary qualities, that is, that some sense qualities appear to be primary or more elemental, and the cause of other sense qualities (secondary qualities). In explaining this, Aristotle borrowed from Empedocles' (495–430 BCE) idea that the basic elements that made up the physical universe were water, air, earth, and fire. Those basic elements produce the primary qualities of wet, dry, cold, and hot. Secondary qualities, things like texture, color, taste, smell, etc., were the result of the primary qualities being arranged in different proportions. All this speculation was limited to the level of what we could experience with our unaided senses. Suddenly, however, the microscope was allowing us to have experiences that went beyond our ordinary senses and we needed some way to account for what we were experiencing on that level.

Although the elements of water, air, earth, and fire seem to be primary regarding the world of our everyday experience, they did not seem to be present on the microscopic level. Of course, since we had never previously experienced that level, there were no words or concepts to describe what we were experiencing there. Since we had no words to describe the microscopic level of experience, we had to invent a nomenclature. The word that seventeenth century thinkers settled on was Aristotle's nondescript term, *matter*. In Aristotle's philosophy matter played a minor role. He never tells us what matter actually is, other than that it is what individuates the Aristotelian forms and allows for members of a species or form to be different from one another, while still being members of the same species. For Aristotle, matter played no role in establishing a thing's form or species, but our understanding of matter took on a very different nature thanks to the microscope.

Many of the great 17th century thinkers (e.g., Rene Descartes, John Locke, Galileo Galilei, Isaac Newton, and Robert Boyle, just to mention a few) championed a new way to understand the idea of matter. They originally referred to this new way of conceptualizing matter as the "corpuscular philosophy" or "corpuscular hypothesis," but this new concept of matter would eventually evolve into modern atomic chemistry. It was very different from Aristotle's nondescript matter, which merely individuated members of a species. The new idea of matter clearly had observable characteristics, and, although there was some disagreement among corpuscularians concerning the list of primary qualities that were being observed on the microscopic level, most agreed at least upon extension, shape, motion, rest, and number. These were the characteristics of what was actually observable on the microscopic level. The philosophical question was how to create an understanding or perspective that could explain and account for this new level of microscopic experience.

The speculation that arose was that perhaps the arrangement and motion of this microscopic matter was the ultimate cause of what we sense on the level of everyday experience. Perhaps the true primary elements were not water, air, earth, and fire but microscopic matter whose arrangement and motion produced all that we experience. Such speculation would lead to a very different picture of the world. With phlogiston chemistry, the basic elements of water, air, earth, and fire were very different kinds of things. With the new corpuscular philosophy, however, there was only one kind of thing: matter. Of course, matter had qualities just like the basic elements of phlogiston chemistry, but the qualities of the new corpuscular philosophy were not like the qualities of wet, dry, cold, and hot. Water and air are two very different kinds of things just as earth and fire are, but corpuscular philosophy's explanation of the microscopic level was that there was only matter. Notice that the qualities that make up the corpuscularians' notion of matter (i.e., extension, shape, motion, rest, and number) are parts of the same thing. This gave rise to a radically different way to conceptualize the world.

In Aristotle's world, something like a thing's color or odor existed within the thing itself and was produced by the basic elements and their qualities arranged in certain combinations to produce that color or odor. The corpuscular philosophy, however, went in a different direction and argued that secondary qualities like colors or odors were not in the thing at all but rather were in us and produced in us by the mechanical arrangement and motion of microscopic matter. The same was true of other secondary sense qualities like taste or sound, which exist in us and not as such within the thing itself. In fact, the only things that exist within the thing itself are the primary qualities that make up matter.

Thus, in answer to the old question of whether a tree falling in the forest made a noise if no one is in the forest, Aristotle would answer yes, since he imagined that what we observe to be in a thing is actually in that thing. The corpuscularians of the modern period, however, would answer, no. They would agree that the tree fell whether there was anyone there or not, because motion was a primary quality to the corpuscularians and existed in the tree itself because the corpuscles that made up the tree possessed motion. They believed, however, that the sound of the tree falling was a secondary quality that only existed in us. The tree really did move and that motion created subsequent motion in the form of waves, but they do not become *sound* until they reach a creature capable of perceiving sound. There is no sound, as such, within the tree itself. Sound only exists in a subject capable of perceiving that motion as sound. Thus, corpuscularians reduced the world to matter alone, and something very different from the world that we actually experience.

Furthermore, for the Aristotelians, the world that we experience consisted of a great variety of different kinds of things and we knew that world through a biological paradigm that conceived of nearly everything as possessing and moved by anima, or soul.

Advent of the Modern Mind: Corpuscular Philosophy

The corpuscularians, on the other hand saw a world made up of one thing: matter, which moves because of mechanical laws. For Aristotle, things were the way they were, and changed the way they did, because of the individual life within them. Everything had its own specific form or nature and behaved according to it. Likewise, we had to study and understand nature according to these specific forms. For the corpuscularians, on the other hand, things changed not because they moved toward a *telos* or purpose built into their species, but because of universal mechanical laws operating on the microscopic level.

With the materialism of corpuscular philosophy, a mechanical paradigm replaced Aristotle's biological model. It was no longer that the world was full of a vast variety of things all with their own form or nature. Instead, the world was mechanical and everything followed the same mechanical laws that governed the material microstructures on this newly discovered level of experience. Unlike Aristotle's world where things were drawn toward ends that were part of their specific form, the corpuscularians saw things being driven by microscopic mechanisms, much like a clock. Such a mechanical rather than biological paradigm made the world much more conducive to being quantified, and understood through universal, mathematical concepts.

A mechanical universe was far less mysterious than a world that moved according to God-infused souls. Such a mechanical model offered the hope that if we could figure out how things mechanically work on the corpuscular level, we can more accurately predict the way things would behave and therein gain greater control over our lives. Of course, Aristotle's science was interested in predicting nature as well. A science that understood the end or purpose toward which a thing moved was predictable. A mechanical universe, however, offered more than mere predictability. Since a machine is without a God-established end, but does what it does because of its mechanical structure, if we can understand that structure, we can theoretically not only predict how a thing will behave, but we can also alter its behavior to our liking.

This was not possible with Aristotelian science by which we discovered how the world worked and then adapted ourselves to that reality. Within a mechanical universe, we no longer needed to adapt ourselves to God's design, but now had the hope of adapting nature to our design. The project was no longer to understand nature but to master and alter it. By altering the mechanical (i.e., chemical or genetic) structure of things, we can determine a thing's end or purpose. Thus, human beings in the modern period were motivated in a way unlike their ancient or medieval predecessors. If God is no longer the sole determiner of ends, we might have the power to alter God's creation in a way that had been previously inconceivable.

One way to understand this is that in the ancient and medieval world science was purely a matter of discovery, while in the modern world science was increasingly a matter of invention. Today, we find it easy to imagine that the things we invent are somehow natural. We see technology as science in a way that the ancient and medieval world would have found unimaginable. Take, for example, the case of Leonardo da Vinci (1452–1519). For years, Leonardo had studied flying. Birds in flight fascinated him, and he desired to understand flying as it exists in nature. At one point, he designed a machine that would simply screw itself into the air.

Some historians speculate that if he had taken time to develop this primitive helicopter, it would have been a heavier than air object that would have gotten off the ground four hundred years before the Wright brothers actually accomplished that in the twentieth century. The reason he did not bother to develop the machine was that he lacked a modern, anthropocentric perspective. The medieval perspective was theocentric; that is, they wanted to discover the order that God had built into nature. What Leonardo wanted was to understand natural flying or flying the way the birds fly. Of course, once we begin to see nature as mechanical, it is easy to imagine that our technology and its machines are natural, and thus scientific. The modern mind would say that helicopters or rockets fly because they are working within the parameters of natural law. The medieval notion of natural meant to replicate or copy nature. To the Aristotelian, medieval mind, flying was an Aristotelian natural form that we would have to discover if we wished to truly fly rather than create some mechanism that overcomes gravity. Once we begin to see nature as mechanical, rather than teleological, we can declare that our machines fly because they conform to mechanical laws that govern the entire universe. Thus, as we came to understand the world mechanically, the distinction between science and technology became blurred and the two became synonymous in our thinking. When we invent the computer, we have no problem imagining that the human brain must be like a computer. We invent a mechanical heart and then imagine that the human heart is simply a machine or part of a machine like our invention. Where the ancient and medieval world would have seen a great distinction between science and technology, the modern world has come to see little or no difference between the two.

This new understanding of the world made the modern mind very different from the ancient/medieval mind that preceded it. Plato and Aristotle focused on the form of things, with matter playing a limited role, while the modern materialism of corpuscular philosophy places matter center stage. But there is more to the story of why it took center stage. Indeed, the corpuscular philosophy provided much more than simply a new way to understand primary and secondary qualities due to the invention of the microscope. The reason behind the popularity of corpuscular philosophy was that it offered the possibility of a mathematical physics in a way that Aristotle thought was impossible.

The ancient Greeks considered the possibility of a mathematical physics or a science of nature as precise as mathematics, but both Plato and Aristotle believed that such an understanding of nature was out of reach. Recall that Plato had hoped to model his philosophy after geometry because the concepts that geometry dealt with were immutable and eternal. In the early dialogues, there is hope that a certain type of philosophical dialogue can bring us to ethical concepts that are eternal and immutable, resembling those of geometry and mathematics, and therein creating a perfect science. In the late dialogues, however, Plato's optimism vanished and he no longer thought that a science of morality after the model of mathematics was possible.

Aristotle also contemplated the possibility of a perfect science, but in the area of physics. He concluded that a mathematical physics or perfect science of the natural world was impossible for two reasons. The first reason was that the natural world was composed of many different forms or natural species. Trees had a different form and therefore were a different kind of thing than

Advent of the Modern Mind: Corpuscular Philosophy   27

rocks or squirrels. With the Aristotelian forms, a mathematical physics was impossible because mathematics works only when we have only one kind of thing. We can add, subtract, multiple, or divide only when we have all members of the same species: three apples plus four apples equals seven apples, but three pears plus four peaches is not quantifiable. Likewise, if the basic elements are water, air, earth, and fire, the basic stuff is not quantifiable. Mathematics requires a single form and does not work between forms, as was necessary when dealing with Aristotle's view of the world. What corpuscular philosophy did was to reduce everything to a single form—matter—thus, overcoming one of Aristotle's objections to the idea of a mathematical physics.

It may appear that the world is made up of different kinds of things, as Aristotle had imagined, but according to the modern materialism of corpuscular philosophy, everything is reducible to mere matter, and matter only differs in quantity and not quality. For the corpuscular philosophy and later the atomic chemistry that grew out of it, all matter is the same and what differentiates gold from hydrogen is that the one has a different quantity of electrons and protons than the other, but all the protons and electrons are the same kind of thing. Since all electrons and protons are the same kind of thing, they differ only in quantity. If gold simply has more of the same basic matter as hydrogen, then a purely quantitative or mathematical understanding of the world is possible. Having reduced all of nature to a single form (matter), modern thinkers took a huge step toward establishing a mathematical physics, but even with that step, there remained yet another problem: how could we be certain that the new science was truly replicating nature? This was Aristotle's second objection to the idea of a mathematical physics.

Aristotle believed that a perfect science or mathematical physics would have to guarantee a match between our understanding of nature and nature itself. Of course, his active intellect gave us the belief that we had knowledge of natural kinds or the forms, but he was also aware of an inherent difference between the way we think about nature and the way we experience it. Perhaps this goes back to the influence of Heraclitus and Parmenides, or perhaps it was a matter of Aristotle's trust that language replicated reality. In the Greek language, there were two words or concepts for time, which reflected the difference between the way we experience time and the way we think about time. *Kairos* was natural time or time as we experienced it, while *khronos* was time as we think about it. Regarding time as we experience it, however, there are not three elements of time but only one: the present. We never experience past or future moments but only present moments. With *khronos*, or how we think about time, however, there is only a past and future, and the present disappears. With *khronos* or sequential time, we are free to create nominal, temporal concepts that have no corresponding reality within nature. Unlike days and years, which have some reference to nature, hours, minutes, and seconds are completely arbitrary. We could have divided the day into one hundred hours, each with one hundred minutes, and each minute with one hundred seconds. Since *khronos* or counting time is arbitrary, we can create ever-smaller units of time and, in so doing, the present can become so infinitesimally small that it disappears and we are left with only past and future. Thus, while time, as we experience it (*kairos*), only exists in the present, and the only day we have ever experienced is today, just as the only year we have ever experienced is this year, time as we think about it (*khronos*) is very different and is essentially a sequence of past and future moments.

Aristotle was aware of this difference between the world as we experience it and the world as we think about it and concluded that a perfect science would have to guarantee such a match between the way we think about nature and the way we experience it. Although the medieval Aristotelians made no pretense to a mathematical physics, they did find at least a limited confidence that they had achieved such a match between their understanding and their experience of nature with the theological belief that God was not a deceiver. If God had given us our empirical senses, and God was not a deceiver, then our senses could be trusted. Furthermore, Aristotle's way of thinking about things was the way we experienced them. That worked with Aristotle's physics but not with the new corpuscular philosophy, since God had not equipped us with senses capable of knowing the microscopic level on which God did actually organize the world, according to the corpuscularians. Thus, how could we be sure that the new mathematical physics replicated nature? If our senses could no longer be trusted, we would need some other basis for guaranteeing that our understanding of the world was in fact true. One option was to believe that God had adequately equipped us, but it was with *reason* rather than our empirical senses and an active intellect. Modern rationalists would argue that it was reason, after the model of mathematics, that made us different from the rest of the animal kingdom, and it was reason that God intended us to use to bring us to an ultimate knowledge of this world. We will explore this in more detail in a later chapter.

Isaac Newton (1643–1727), however, offered a better solution to Aristotle's second objection concerning a match between the way we think about nature and the way we experience it. Newton was a corpuscularian but made his enormous contribution to modern science with his mathematical calculations concerning several natural phenomena, which he then validated with experiments that confirmed those calculations in experience. Although perhaps not exactly what Aristotle had in mind, it was enough to assure most modern thinkers that our new mathematical science did indeed replicate the world as we experience it.

In addition to the match between our thinking about the world and our experience of the world, there was another match that the medieval mind thought essential. That other match was between our understanding of the world and the actual order that God had built into nature. This was at the base of the theocentric perspective, which sought to understand things from God's perspective. Aristotle's active intellect had given us some confidence that we had a least a basis for such a match, but now that confidence was lost. If the corpuscular philosophy was right and natural kinds emanated from the microscopic level, we lost Aristotle's basis for such a connection to the natural world and the anthropocentric view seemed our only option. We will deal with this matter and our modern quest to know natural kinds in a later chapter, but for now, it is enough to understand that an enormous shift from a theocentric to an anthropocentric perspective was underway. This shift in our thinking further blurred the distinction between science and technology, in that we no longer sought to discover God's understanding of flying but we conceptualized flying in a way that would allow us to fly. There are no helicopters in nature and the humming bird cannot fly according to our theories of aerodynamics, but that is not a problem to the modern mind. Today, computer science is termed a science but it does not seek to replicate nature in any direct way. Yet, strangely, once we invented the computer, many of us naively imagined that we had finally discovered how the human mind works. With the anthropocentric view, human beings became the measure of all things, and God and nature lost their preeminence. If rockets fly, science has become technology and the philosophical imagination is freer than it was in the ancient and medieval world. We would see little problem with this until the twentieth century when ecological concerns caused us to question the wisdom of pursuing an anthropocentric technology largely divorced from nature.

CHAPTER THREE

Immaterialists: Gottfried Wilhelm Leibniz and George Berkeley

The new materialism of corpuscular philosophy and its mechanical view of the universe dominated the modern period and went a long way in creating the nature of the modern mind. As dominant as this thinking became, however, it was not without opposition, and several 17th and 18th century thinkers took a serious stand against this emerging concept of matter. Two of the most famous of these immaterialists were the German philosopher and mathematician Gottfried Wilhelm Leibniz (1646–1716) and the Irish philosopher George Berkeley (1685–1753).

Both Leibniz and Berkeley considered the idea of matter literally nonsense. If it sounds ridiculous to deny the existence of matter, it is because matter is a concept that we inherit as part of our modern perspective and, as such, it goes largely unexamined. Leibniz and Berkeley, however, did consider the idea of matter and they pointed out that no one has ever experienced matter as the corpuscularians imagined it. Consider the fact that there can never be any empirical evidence for our modern concept of matter, since modern materialists claimed that matter was something more than sensations and the very thing that caused sensations. The immaterialists argued that all we can ever know are sensations and there can never be any empirical evidence for whatever creates sensations or the images that make up the world of our experience. Against the immaterialists, the materialists argued that something must create sensations and *matter* was the best explanation. The immaterialists, on the other hand, contended that God created the sensate world and it was more reasonable to believe that a divine mind creates the sensations and the images that make up the world of our experience, rather than inorganic matter.

We all experience our own minds creating sensations and images in dreams and can even muster up sensations when awake as well, but nothing in our experience leads us to believe that inorganic matter can create ideas, sensations, or images. Thus, the immaterialists argued that it was more reasonable to believe that a divine mind more substantial and enduring than our own was responsible for the images and sensations that make up the world of our experience. The corpuscularians, for fear of offending the church and being accused of heresy, which could have meant torture or death, maintained that God had empowered matter to create sensations and then set physical laws in place in order to govern how matter mechanically functioned. The immaterialists claimed that God had created sensations directly, rather than through the intermediate medium of matter.

Most immaterialists imagined that if we accepted the idea of matter as the cause of the sensate world, it would lead to deism or even atheism. Deism was the growing modern belief that God had created the world but was no longer present and no longer intervened in human affairs. If God had created a material world that was self-sustaining, God could even cease to exist or otherwise lose interest in the world and the world would continue in God's absence. For the deists, God was merely a creator of the universe and that was the extent of the Divine's involvement. Seeing this as a threat to their Christianity, Leibniz and Berkeley developed philosophical perspectives that required God to play a larger role than creating a material world that operated according to purely mechanical laws. Beyond seeing the new materialism as a threat to Christianity, both Leibniz and Berkeley had other problems with it as well.

Leibniz, in addition to being a philosopher, was also a world class mathematician and invented or developed modern calculus, although there is a famous dispute over whether Leibniz or Isaac Newton was the true inventor of modern calculus. The most respected position is that the two invented calculus independently of one another and, although the English insist it was Newton and the Germans side with Leibniz, the rest of Europe preferred Leibniz's version throughout the modern period. As much as Leibniz and Newton shared the same ideas concerning calculus, their ideas concerning other things were at enormous odds. While Newton was a corpuscularian and champion of materialism, Leibniz was an immaterialist.

For Leibniz, the idea of material corpuscles, or atoms as they would later come to be known, was irrational since such a theory required not only the existence of matter but equally the existence of the *void* as well. If matter was to be capable of motion, there would have to exist a void or nothingness into which matter would be capable of moving. If nothing but matter existed then matter would have to be motionless, but if the void existed along with matter in order to allow for motion, that meant that something, which was nothing, existed. To say that *nothing* exists, Leibniz considered a blatant contradiction.

Consequently, Leibniz offered an alternative explanation for what the corpuscularians had speculated we were experiencing on the microscopic level. Leibniz began by arguing that what had been found on the microscopic level were not bits of matter, but rather monads. A monad was Leibniz' name for what he would use to replace matter in his explanation of the microscopic world. A monad was a soul or metaphysical point into which God programed all of the perceptions that a particular monad would contain and emit over time. These monads did not affect one another and Leibniz tells us they are windowless, without any causal interaction between them. Since the entire physical universe was made-up of monads and nothing but monads, there was no void, which meant that the motion of one monad required that all the other monads in the universe would have to move as well. Thus, in creating the world, God not only put together these monads and the perceptions they would emit, but he also coordinated the motion of these monads, since the motion of one monad required all the other monads in the universe to move as well. Thus, God created a world of such enormous complexity that it is hard to imagine how such a task could be accomplished, and of course, that is at least part of Leibniz' point: that the world that God created is beyond our comprehension and hardly one that can be reduced to mechanical laws that we can understand.

For Leibniz, the changes we experience in the world are not the result of mechanical causes, but are the direct result of God's will. For Leibniz, there are no mechanical or secondary causes in the physical universe; God is the cause of everything in the physical realm. Unlike the corpuscularians who believed that God created matter and then matter and mechanical laws governed nature, Leibniz believed that God was the sole cause of nature and there was no material intermediary. For Leibniz, everything that happens in the physical universe, including our behavior, is the direct result of God's will and reasoning. Consequently, the physical universe is determined, just as the materialists had hoped, but it is not mechanically determined in a way that we can figure out and perhaps alter. Leibniz's world is determined by a divine mind whose reasoning is beyond our comprehension.

Leibniz's work may appear strange to us, but that is largely due to how deeply embedded is our inherited prejudice toward a materialist understanding of the world. If we can suspend that prejudice for a moment, we can discover that Leibniz offers an interesting perspective that is closer to a twenty-first century understanding of the world than it was to a seventeenth century understanding. For one thing, the corpuscular philosophy of the seventeenth century saw causality as mechanical and linear. One gear moves because another gear moved it. Today, however, chaos theory suggests that such a linear picture of causal correlations is not an adequate way to think about causality. In fact, multiple factors are usually behind the events we experience in the physical world and, in the great scheme of things, a butterfly flapping its wings in China has a causal correlation to a hurricane in the Caribbean five months later. Of course, trying to think to that level of complexity causes our minds to overload and our imagination fails. Likewise, it is difficult to imagine the kind of causal connections that Leibniz imagines God calculated in creating the universe. Certainly, corpuscular philosophy represented a much simpler view of the universe. Indeed, it represents a view of the universe that makes the universe understandable to our limited imagination. Of course, a twenty-first century scientific view is much more complex than the view of early modern science, although it still does not even approach the kind of complexity of which Leibniz speaks. That degree of complexity may not be imaginable for centuries.

Another aspect of Leibniz's thought that was not compatible with the thinking of his day, but has more in common with the thinking of our day, is his idea of free will. At first, it might appear that Leibniz denies the idea of free will entirely, since God determines everything that happens in the physical universe, and human beings have no hand in determining even their own behavior. Yet Leibniz does claim that human beings are free. His idea of freedom is rather complex and more than we would want to take on here, but it essentially involves the idea of volition. Put in simplest terms, his idea of volition seems to connote something like participation. It is a willingness to accept one's fate and attempt to see how our circumstance fits with God's greater purpose. To put Leibniz in terms that would make sense to a twenty-first century mind, human freedom, although not existing on the physical level where God determines everything, does exist regarding how we interpret our physical reality. Today we understand, better than our early modern ancestors did, that there is a difference between the physical circumstances of our lives and the way we interpret those circumstances. Although our DNA, behavioral conditioning, or habitual conformity to social norms may determine our physical circumstances, there is a freedom available because we can interpret those circumstances in a variety of ways. In the same

Immaterialists: Gottfried Leibniz and George Berkeley 39

way, Leibniz's physical world is completely determined by God, but we are free to interpret those circumstances as we wish. Our philosophical imagination gives us enormous freedom regarding how we wish to interpret the physical circumstances of our lives. Do we see our circumstances as a blessing or a curse? Can we see beauty in our circumstances or only despair? Our lives are still largely in our own hands even if every minute physical detail and circumstance is determined.

Leibniz also offered another interesting argument against materialism with his famous mill analogy. Materialists have tried to reduce everything, including the human mind, down to a material brain that functions mechanically. Leibniz's argument against such a notion is that even if we could trace mental states to a mechanical causal chain, we would be at a loss to explain what initiated the chain. He uses the example of a mill that operates mechanically whereby one gear moves another. In such a mill, however, something outside the mill (namely the water from a flowing river) must initiate the movement of the first gear. Likewise, trying to reduce the mind to a material brain that functions according to mechanical laws would still need something outside the mechanism in order to initiate it, just as the mill needs something outside of the machine itself to initiate the mechanism. Even if we can trace thoughts to mechanical activity in the brain, the question remains: What initiates that mechanical chain when we do something willfully that is not a response to some physical stimulus?

The fact that Leibniz constantly points to the fact that things are more mysterious than the materialists would like to believe has caused some scholars to consider Leibniz a mystic. Others see his strong leanings toward mathematics as evidence against considering him a mystic, but many famous mathematicians, including Pythagoras and Pascal, were also mystics. Whether he was a mystic or not is hard to say, but he certainly presented a view of the world that was more mysterious than the materialists' view and he serves as a great example of the philosophical imagination at work.

The part of Leibniz's philosophy that perhaps has received the most criticism over the years has been his explanation for why God chose to program the world as he has. His explanation is also his answer to the problem of evil: that is, why did an omnibenevolent, omnipotent, omniscient, sole creator create a world with so much evil and suffering? Leibniz's answer to these questions is that God chose to program and organize all of physical reality in the way he did because he wanted to create the best of all possible worlds. Leibniz argues that in creating the world, God considered an infinite number of possible worlds, and then chose to create this world because it was the best possible. God could have created an infinite number of worlds, many of which could have had little or no evil and suffering, but such worlds would equally eliminate certain divine elements like forgiveness, mercy, and compassion, which require the presence of evil and suffering.

Berkeley

Another important immaterialist of the early modern period was the Irish philosopher, George Berkeley (1685–1753). Like Leibniz, his immaterialism was a reaction to the materialism of corpuscular philosophy, but he differed from Leibniz on several points. Like Leibniz, he thought that the idea of matter was nonsense, but unlike Leibniz, Berkeley was not interested in housing perceptions in monads. For Berkeley only two types of things existed: ideas and the minds that create them. By ideas, Berkeley means something different than what we normally take to be ideas. To Berkeley, ideas are perceptions or images, and they along with the minds that create or perceive them are the only things that exist. John Locke (1632–1704), who was a believer in corpuscular philosophy, had made a similar move in questioning Aristotle's idea of material substance. For the medieval Aristotelians, a material substance was the insensible thing that united and held together the sense qualities of a substance. Although a rabbit might be brown in color, furry, and have a certain shape, what made all of those sense qualities hang together and move as a single entity was its substance, which Aristotelians imagined held the sense qualities together. This substance, which held the sense qualities together, was itself insensible, which caused an empiricist like Locke to say that a material substance was a thing "...we know not what." A material substance was unknowable to Locke, since he maintained that all we can ever know are ideas and, for Locke, all ideas have their origin in experience. Having no experience of the substance that holds the sense qualities together, we can have no idea of it, and therefore no knowledge of it. Thus, we should consider a thing that "we know not what" as no thing at all. Of course, a similar situation existed with matter of which we equally have no experience. Since Berkeley thought that only minds and their ideas (i.e., images or perceptions) exist, he found it unimaginable to introduce a third kind of thing (matter), which was neither a mind nor an idea, but somehow had the power to create ideas even though it was not a mind.

We personally experience our own minds creating ideas or perception, and we can see the ideas or perceptions that God's mind creates, but we have no experience of this occult notion of matter creating perceptions. Matter was neither mind nor something that we could perceive. Since the materialists believed that matter was the cause of what we perceive, it could not have been a perception itself, but neither was it mind. Thus, Berkeley dismissed it as an occult quality. Earlier, Isaac Newton had been accused of dabbling in the occult with his work on gravity, since gravity was neither a mind nor something that could be sensed. Newton was able to defend himself by pointing out that gravity was not a thing at all but a mathematical relationship or formula. Of course, Newton could not use that in defense of his idea of matter, which was not a relationship but a thing that was neither mind nor a perception. This, along with the fact that Berkeley could not imagine how inanimate and insensible matter could have the power to create the sensate world, was the basis of Berkeley's attack on materialism.

In order to understand Berkeley, we have to begin with the fact that human minds can both receive and project images or perceptions (ideas). In dreams our minds project images, so why not believe that the images we see in our waking hours are simply the projection of a mind much greater than our own? In dreams, our minds create all the images that appear there, and there are no causal connections between the images. The dreamer is the sole cause of all that happens there. If one dreams of a witch rolling down a hill and hitting an apple tree, and an apple falls and hits her in the head, the cause of the apple hitting her in the head was the dreamer and not the fact that she actually hit the tree with enough force to make the apple fall. Just as we are the only cause in our dreams and there are no secondary causes within them, Berkeley thought the same was true of the natural world, which was a projection of God's mind in the same way that our dreams are projections of our own minds. Berkeley went on to argue that this world, which is a projection of God's mind, is in fact a divine language through which God communicated to us.

Berkeley's world is made up of no more than ideas or perceptions that have no causal power, just as there was no causal power within Leibniz's world. Beyond that, however, the two immaterialists are quite different. One of the big differences is that Berkeley claimed that God had given us sovereignty over our limbs. Thus, human beings were able to interact with the sensate world and thereby transform the natural sensations of God's creation into houses, bridges, and a great multitude of artifacts.

Berkeley's immaterialism is also simpler and easier to grasp than Leibniz's. At the heart of Berkeley's rejection of materialism is corpuscular philosophy's concept of matter as a causal agent. Berkeley found it impossible to imagine how matter, which was not an idea, nor a mind, could create ideas. On the other hand, he found it easy to imagine how minds create ideas or perceptions since our minds create perceptions and images both in dreams and in our waking hours. Since our minds are able to create perceptions and sensate images, why would we not think that the sensations that make up the world are equally the direct creation of a mind rather than the creation of dead matter? Unlike our own minds, however, the mind or spirit that is responsible for the perceptions and images that make up the natural world is a mind much greater in power and faithfulness than our own. While our minds create ideas or images that are flimsy and fleeting, God's mind creates much more substantial images, and his faithfulness makes them more consistent and enduring than the images our minds are able to muster. While the materialists imagined that mechanical laws governed the material world, Berkeley thought that the consistency we see in the natural world was the result of God's faithfulness, rather than mechanical laws.

Berkeley did not attack the idea of matter solely because it was nonsensical, however. He also attacked it on a theological level and accused the materialists of idolatry. To Berkeley, claiming that inanimate matter somehow had the power to create sensations seemed a blatant form of idolatry, and represented a serious threat to Christianity. He saw the materialism of the modern era as laying the foundation for deism and eventually atheism. Indeed, if God created matter and then matter created the sensible world, such an intermediary between God and the world of our experience meant that God's creation was somewhat independent of him. This allowed the deists to argue that God may have created the world but there is no reason to believe that God continued to interact with the world, since the world was capable of functioning on its own and could continue in God's absence.

The materialists did win the day and we moderns became materialists rather than immaterialists, but it is interesting to consider what caused us to go in that direction rather than toward the immaterialism of Leibniz or Berkeley. The understanding through which we conceptualize and interpret our experience is always philosophical rather than scientific simply because science deals with what is out there, while philosophy deals with what is in us, and through which we interpret what is out there. We need a philosophical perspective before we can begin to make sense of what is out there. We rarely consider the inherited understanding through which we interpret the world as philosophical, since we receive it as an inheritance in childhood, but whatever perspective we inherit originated out of someone's philosophical imagination and not out of science *per se*. Science may give support for a philosophical perspective but it cannot create a philosophical perspective. That can only come about through the philosophical imagination. Once generated, however, there are reasons why we accept one philosophical perspective and not another. There were several reasons that the materialists rather than the immaterialists won the day and our modern philosophical perspective became that of the materialists. For one thing, the materialism of corpuscular philosophy gave us a mathematical physics and the sense of security that comes from believing that our knowledge is certain and precise, like mathematics. A second reason for the modern era moving toward materialism was that a mechanical world governed by laws of nature gave us the idea that nature was more predictable and safer than a world created and governed by a Divine sovereign. In political philosophy, there was a similar move toward a rule of law rather than rule by a divinely appointed sovereign. Yet another factor that led to the dominance of materialism over immaterialism was that if we could gain knowledge of the mechanical laws that governed the material world, we could alter it to our liking. That was not possible in a world governed by God's faithfulness rather than mechanical laws.

These factors certainly contributed to the materialist victory, but another factor was that many religious types were averse to immaterialism. The religious and theological atmosphere of the modern period was becoming more comfortable with a rational rather than a mysterious faith. What was especially attractive to many religious types was that the new materialism gave them an answer to "the problem of evil" that they found preferable to the immaterialists' treatment of the problem. A materialist could argue that although God was an all-good, all-powerful, and all-knowing sole creator, evil was not God's responsibility since God had created a material, mechanical world that was without evil in its original form but human sin brought evil into the world which corrupted the world that God had created. Thus, God was not culpable for the evil and suffering we see in the world.

With the immaterialists, however, that was not an option, since God was the direct cause of the sensate world. Of course, Berkeley's immaterialism was not as distasteful as Leibniz's, since, according to Berkeley, God had given us sovereignty over our limb,; so that evil and suffering could be attributed to human beings rather than God. God, however, was still responsible for natural disasters and events where human action was not involved. As religion became more rational and less mystical in the modern era, a philosophical perspective that gave us a rational explanation that would exonerate God from having caused evil and suffering was attractive. The materialists seem to have done a better job at exonerating God as the cause of evil, but that is largely because most religious people want a God who conforms to their idea of goodness. The immaterialists, however, seem to see a Divinity that transcends our idea of goodness. This is especially true of Berkeley who must have had a deeper spirituality than one founded upon human notions of goodness. His wife Anne is reported to have said, "He was a God-intoxicated man." Several of the events of his life seem to bear this out, but none more than something that happened in his old age. Berkeley had several children but he had a son in his old age that he particularly loved. He spent most of his time with the child, overseeing his education and delighting in his music. When the child was nine years old, he died and Berkeley was devastated. In a touching letter to another Anglican Bishop in the south of Ireland, Berkeley speaks of how much he loved the child, but concludes the letter with the line, "But God in his infinite mercy took him from me."

Berkeley seems to have been able to see mercy in an event that most of us would find impossible to describe as merciful. Perhaps the immaterialist perspective allows for a different way of interpreting events. Both Leibniz and Berkeley seemed to have had a more mystical faith that put them at odds with much of our increasingly rational, modern thinking. What appears to have really distinguished immaterialists like Leibniz and Berkeley from other thinkers of the period was that they resisted the temptation to think of themselves as enlightened and continued to stand in humble awe before a universe that far exceeded their capacity to understand.

CHAPTER FOUR

The Kinds Problem: Rene Descartes and John Locke

If the materialism of corpuscular philosophy was going to replace Aristotle's philosophical perspective, the philosophical imagination had to deal with the problem of natural kinds. Words with the exception of pronouns and personal nouns are not about individual things. Our words signify concepts or entire classes of things. The medieval Aristotelians believed we knew the natural kinds to which words refer because of a God-given active intellect. Of course, that was just Aristotle justifying or providing some rational account to support a natural prejudice that results from the fact that everyone in our language community has learned to conceptualize the world in the same way because of the commonality of a particular language. With age, some people become more cosmopolitan and realize that there are other ways of conceptualizing the world. That was not generally the case in the medieval world, where most people were without books and travel was limited. For most people there was nothing to unseat their initial prejudices and they imagined that the world was as they had learned to conceptualize it through the acquisition of language.

We learn of kinds through the acquisition of language and, if nothing challenges those concepts, our prejudices concerning them remain intact. The microscope and ensuing corpuscular philosophy made us suspicious of those prejudices. If the matter that existed on the microscopic level was the cause of what we experienced on the level of everyday experience, perhaps it was the microscopic level, and not Aristotelian forms, that determined natural kinds. Consequently, corpuscularians lost their confidence in Aristotle's active intellect to give us access to the actual kinds of things that existed within nature. Perhaps things like gold or water were not the kinds of things they were because they shared a common Aristotelian forms but because of microstructures like Au_{79} and H_2O. Similarly, we would eventually classify animal and plant species into kinds by their genetic makeup rather than perceived Aristotelian forms. Thus, in the absence of an active intellect, early corpuscularians faced the challenge of coming up with new ways of conceptualizing natural kinds.

Several options were possible. One was the option of the deists who believed that God did little more than create the world and now it was up to us to figure out how best to live in it. The rise of deism and later atheism meant we were on our own to organize the world into kinds that best suited our human purposes. The problem was a little different for theists who wanted to maintain that God had equipped us to know the world as he had created it, or for those who were afraid of the church and its Inquisition charging them with heresy for following the path of the deists. The French philosopher and mathematician Rene Descartes (1596–1650) suggested a solution that he hoped would satisfy both groups.

Since Descartes was in France, the threat of the Inquisition was a serious matter. Galileo (1564–1642) had recently faced the Inquisition for his support of Copernicus' idea of a heliocentric universe, which opposed the church's belief in a geocentric universe. To challenge the accepted thinking of the day was a dangerous thing, and the accepted thinking of the day was still Aristotelian. Thus, Descartes had to tread carefully like many innovative thinkers in times when it was not healthy to be an innovator. We must read Descartes between the lines. He is careful to introduce his new notion of kinds, while not upsetting the sensibilities of the Inquisition. In fact, he does not even address the question of kinds, but that is the clear implication of all he has to say; if accused, he could defend himself by arguing that he is nowhere offering an alternative to Aristotle. He mentions that he was thinking of writing another book, *Le Monde* (The World), but recent developments (Galileo's trial) made him think it best to write another book instead which was about his own thinking process rather than the world itself. If accused of heresy, he could argue that he was not talking about the world and the way Aristotle and the church conceived it, but only the way he has found useful to organize his own thoughts. Of course, the book can be read in other ways as well, and Descartes is a master at writing on these multiple levels. For the church, he is only writing about a way to organize his own thoughts. To those who want to find how God actually organized the world if it were not through Aristotelian forms, Descartes can be read as suggesting that mathematics and the kind of reasoning at the base of mathematics is the actual way that God has equipped us to understand the world that God created. Finally, for the deist and atheist he is suggesting the best way to organize their experience in the absence of God.

The fact that we can read Descartes' *Discourse on Method* on several different levels is certainly part of his genius. He is introducing a radically different way of thinking about the world while avoiding the ire of the Inquisition. Later generations considered him the father of modern philosophy and he never had to face the Inquisition. That was not an easy thing to pull off. He was very careful not to say that God has given us something better than an active intellect in the form of the kind of reasoning we find in mathematics, but that is the implication, although he can deny ever having said such a thing. Descartes' real genius lay in his introducing a radically different way of viewing the world, while assuring the Church that he was not talking about the world or its kinds at all, but he is merely explaining a method of reasoning that he has personally found useful and others may find useful as well.

This method of reasoning follows the model of mathematics or more particularly geometry (which incidentally, Descartes invented); so in addition to be considered the father of modern philosophy, he is also considered the father of modern analytic geometry. What Descartes found so attractive about mathematics and geometry was that the concepts dealt with were always clear and distinct. There is no doubt about or disagreement over the concept of seven or a circle the way there is disagreement concerning our concepts of things in the world. Thus, like Plato, Descartes believed that mathematics and geometry offered the ideal forms for knowledge. The difference between Plato and Descartes, however, lay in the fact that while Plato wanted to know the ultimate form of things like love, courage, and justice with the same certainty and exactness he knew geometrical and mathematical concepts, Descartes took a very different path. Plato had accepted the cultural concepts he inherited but wanted to know them with the clarity with which we know the definition of a circle or the concept seven. Descartes wanted to create entirely new concepts based not on experience but reason alone. This marked an enormous shift from medieval thinking and another reason many consider Descartes the father of modern philosophy.

Of course, if we were to accept *only* those things of which we could be certain, the senses would no longer be a reliable source of truth, since our senses cannot provide clear and distinct ideas that are certain and beyond doubt. The Aristotelian church trusted our God-given senses and when Galileo claimed that Copernicus was right and the sun did not go around the earth but the earth went around the sun, the church's response was that we see the sun go around the earth with our God-given eyes. Descartes knew that he was putting himself in a similar situation by offering an alternative to our God-given senses. If charged, however, Descartes had an ace up his sleeve and could argue that his clear and distinct ideas were clear and distinct because they were innate or God-given. It is hard to know whether Descartes actually believed that, or if he was merely setting up a possible defense if charged by the Inquisition. If all clear and distinct ideas were certain because they were innate and God-given, the Church of the Inquisition would have a harder time convicting Descartes of heresy should such a charge have arisen. In order to avoid Socrates' fate, philosophers through the ages often had to write in ways that were ambiguous enough to leave them a way out if they needed it, and Descartes' circumstances put him in just such a position. It is ironic that although Descartes speaks of clear and distinct ideas, he did not want to be too clear and distinct in his writing for fear of the Church.

On the matter of developing new concepts through which to understand this changing world of the seventeenth century,

Descartes never developed such concepts in his own fifty-four years, but he did try to get us started and showed what he thought would be the method of developing such new concepts or notions of natural kinds through which to organize our understanding. In his *Discourse on Method*, he suggests that we begin by finding some absolutely certain first principle. He had developed or invented analytic geometry by using that same principle. He began with self-evident truths that he claimed were impossible to doubt. For example, the shortest distance between two points being a straight line is a self-evident truth (or at least it was until the idea of a geodesic or a distance of least resistance seemed more in keeping with twentieth century physics). As he did with geometry, Descartes wanted to begin his understanding of things apart from mathematics with the same principle. The self-evident principle he settles on is his famous, "cogito ergo sum" (I think therefore I am). He maintained that as much as he might try to doubt the existence of his own mind, he found that the very act of doubting his mind confirmed its existence (*Dubito ergo sum*—I doubt therefore I am).

Today we have a better understanding that this is more the kind of myth that we need to get our quest for knowledge started rather than some ultimate truth. It is the kind of noble lie that we need to tell ourselves in order to believe that we have some sort of rational foundation for our knowledge. Socrates does the same thing. In Plato's *Meno*, Socrates tells his interlocutor, Meno, a myth about how learning is possible because we had experienced the Platonic forms in a previous existence. Meno is impressed and believes Socrates has just proven that knowledge is possible because the soul existed before our birth into this bodily existence, but Socrates is quick to admit that he is not willing to swear an oath concerning the truth of this myth. The truth to which he is willing to swear an oath, however, is that we will be better and braver human beings if we pursue knowledge,[2] but it appears that knowledge requires a myth to get started.

Descartes makes a similar move. He begins with the noble lie that all clear and distinct ideas are true, but clear and distinct ideas are no more than clear and distinct ideas. All unicorns have one horn is as clear and distinct an idea as all bachelors are unmarried men. Both are beyond doubt but no more than the association of ideas. To define truth in such a way is a huge leap of faith rather than a matter of reason, but some such leap is a necessary starting point for all attempts at knowledge. Descartes demonstrates this in the section of his *Discourse on Method* that immediately precedes the section on the *cogito*. There he presents the moral rules derived from his method. In the second maxim of these rules, he says, "My second maxim was that of being as firm and resolute in my actions as I could be, and not to follow less faithfully opinions the most dubious, when my mind was once made up regarding them, than if these had been beyond doubt."[3] He goes on to use an example of being lost in a forest and not knowing the way out. He says what is best and "very true and very certain"[4] is that we should pick a direction and follow it resolutely without wavering; that is, we should act as if we know even when we do not know.

---

2. Plato. *Meno*. 86b6-8.

3. Descartes, Rene. *Discourse on the Method.* Trans. Elizabeth S. Haldane and G. R. T. Ross. Philosophical Works of Descartes. (Vol. 1) (New York: Dover Publications, Inc. 1955), 96.

4. Idid.

Without that conviction and the resolute action to follow it, we will wander aimlessly. Thus, Descartes' great truth, like Socrates', is that we need a conviction or belief in order to get started on our way toward knowledge. Strangely, this is a truth that is clear and certain, and pragmatically necessary if we are to pursue knowledge. Unfortunately, Descartes' notion of truth may give us the illusion that our foundations really are certain, while in fact, all such foundations are simply a faith in a certain perspective or way of seeing and thinking about things.

Both Socrates and Descartes provide us with the kind of necessary myths that we need to pursue knowledge. The difference between the two seems to rest in the fact that Descartes actually believed or at least wanted us to believe that his starting point of the cogito is an actual rational principle rather than a necessary myth, while Socrates was quick to recognize and acknowledge the mythic nature of where he begins.

Socrates and Plato are far less optimistic in comparison to Descartes (and much of the modern thinking that would follow Descartes) concerning our foundations for knowledge. In Plato's *Theaetetus* Socrates and Theaetetus are trying to come to an understanding (definition) of knowledge. After several failed attempts, they settle on the idea that knowledge is true opinion plus a *logos*; that is, a true opinion plus a reasoned account that supports that true opinion. That is still the definition of knowledge that many use today, but Socrates reminds us that it is less than satisfactory since when we unpack our knowledge all the way back to foundations, we come to words, and even before that letters for which there can be no *logos* or reasoned account. Why is it true that the letter L is the letter L? There is no reasoned account or *logos* to support that. It is simply a convention or agreed upon starting point from which to begin, similar to Descartes being lost in the woods.

We see a similar case with the Logical Positivists of the twentieth century. They were philosophers who demanded verification for truth claims and stated their belief that they would "accept nothing as meaningful unless it could be verified or falsified in observation." Of course, that statement is self-referentially false or meaningless by its own criterion. In other words, we cannot verify or falsify that statement in observation. It is a faith statement like all foundational beliefs. Descartes' foundations are the same. He puts his faith in clear and distinct ideas because he must put his faith in something if he has any hope of getting out of a forest in which he finds himself lost. Certainly, there is truth in what Descartes says. His first principle of acting as if we know even when we do not know is the place from which we all begin. We all need a perspective from which to begin, and it gives us a great sense of security to believe that our perspective is something we know to be true rather than merely a matter of faith. Indeed, as children, it was necessary to our psychological and social well-being to understand our inherited perspective as something we knew and of which we were certain, but with age we should gain the wisdom and courage to face the reality of an existence whose ultimate foundation is faith rather than knowledge.

Locke

Another corpuscularian who had a very different solution to this problem caused by the loss of Aristotle's active intellect was the British philosopher John Locke (1632–1704). Although Locke rejected Aristotle's idea of an active intellect, he approached the question of natural kinds in much the same way that Aristotle and Thomas Aquinas had. Like them, Locke thought that our ideas of kinds came about through a process of abstraction. When we observe several things that all bear the same name, Locke believed that our mind detects and abstracts the common feature or essence that runs through all members of that species or kind. Unlike the Aristotelians, however, Locke believed that this process of abstraction was a matter of judgment rather than the result of an active intellect. As a corpuscularian, Locke believed that the real essence of things existed on the corpuscular level, to which we had limited access in the seventeenth century. Therefore, the essences we abstract with our judgments and to which we attach words are nominal and for the sake of language rather than the real essences that caused things to be the kind of things they were.

In explaining the process by which we form nominal essences in the absence of an active intellect, Locke begins with simple sense data. Recall from the last chapter that Locke rejected the concept of a material substance that held the sense qualities together, and which Locke claimed was a "thing we know not what." Without the idea of a material substance, Locke concluded that sense qualities enter the mind as "simples" as he called them, and we make judgments concerning what sense qualities go together in order to form our ideas of individual substances. We make these judgments based upon the fact that we see some sense qualities constantly conjoined. With animals, the judgments are quite simple since all the sense qualities that make up a something like a rabbit move together. Thus, the judgment that we make concerning the rabbit's furriness, shape, color, etc. being parts of the

The Kinds Problem: Rene Descartes and John Locke   59

same substance seems obvious. With such a judgment, we have very little liberty, in fact so little liberty that it does not even feel like a judgment. Of course, that is only true of visual sense qualities, and we are often mistaken about our judgments concerning sense qualities like sounds or smells belonging to a particular substance. Regarding the judgments we make concerning the visual sense qualities that make up a substance, however, their union hardly seems to be the result of a judgment at all, but Locke insists they are. In the absence of an active intellect to detect substantial forms, judgments are not a bad explanation, especially if we think of them occurring on an unconscious level.

If we consider substantial forms other than animals, it is a little easier to see that they emerge from judgments rather than knowledge. With a substance like a tree, the sense qualities do not all move together and consequently it is a little easier to see that we compile them through judgments. For example, since we generally find the simples that make up the branches conjoined with the simples that make up the leaves, we make a judgment about them belonging to the same substance. Of course, very often we find leaves and branches not conjoined and, for that reason, a judgment is required to put them together in the same substance. Likewise, we find the sense qualities that make up the roots of the tree generally conjoined with the simples that make up the soil, but here we make a different judgment about the sense qualities that make up the roots being of a different substance than the simples that make up the soil. Of course, this too is such a deeply held prejudice that it does not seem to be a judgment at all, until we consider a different people group who imagine that what is above the ground are different kinds of things than what is beneath the ground. For such a people, the tree stops at ground level and does not include the roots.

This matter of how we form ideas of individual substances is interesting but hardly a major concern for Locke. What does concern him is the next level of judgments whereby we put individual substances together into species or kinds of things. This is the critical level since we attach words (with the exception of pronouns and personal nouns) not to individual substances like a tree or a cat, but to kinds of things like trees or cats. Locke, as a corpuscularian, believed that the real essences of things and what caused them to be of one species rather than another existed on the microscopic level. Since we knew little about the microscopic level in Locke's day, we still determined species on the level of everyday experience and attached words to the nominal essences we created out of judgments. Of course, Aristotle believed that this process was performed by an active intellect rather than judgments but, as a corpuscularian, that option was not open to Locke who needed a different explanation for how we formed our ideas of these essences to which we attached words. He too claimed that we abstract an essence from among a specific group, but it was a judgment of the mind rather than the work of an active intellect that performed this abstraction.

For Aristotle, the active intellect created the grouping in the first place; so abstracting an essence to which to attach a name was secondary to the original grouping. Locke's explanation of how we abstract an essence to which to attach a name comes through experience and the judgments that accompany that experience. For example, in a child's first attempts at language, she discovers that the family's Saint Bernard is a *dog*. With that information, the child is very likely to extend that name to all four-legged house pets until some older member of the language community informs her that the smaller house pet is a *cat*. Shortly after learning this and encountering a Yorkie while walking with her mother, she identifies the Yorkie as *cat*. It is only with time and correction that we learn to make the correct judgments and abstract the essence used by other members of the language community. Thus, we learn how to group things into kinds through childhood language acquisition, but the question remains concerning the formation of the original grouping. If it is not an active intellect then what is the basis for it? Locke did not seem too concerned with this question since he believes that the real essence of things, and therefore the real basis for kinds, results from the arrangement and motion of the corpuscles on the microscopic level. Thus, for Locke, the nominal essences and their kinds to which the seventeenth century attached words were little more than social conventions.

Locke was clearly a nominalist in his day because of the limited knowledge of the microscopic level in the seventeenth century. His hope was that in the future, when we have acquired enough knowledge of the microscopic level, we will be able to attach words to those real essences rather than the conventional, nominal essences of his day. Like so many of his contemporary corpuscularians, he believed that in the future we would attach our words and our ideas of kinds to the corpuscular structures that were the real cause of natural kinds. That day did come, but when it did, we had no more of an active intellect on that level than we did on the level of everyday experience; so the essences we created on the microscopic level were still like those we encounter on the level of everyday experience. Of course, on the microscopic level there was no inherited nomenclature or language from which to begin our abstraction; so we were more on our own than ever before to create the groupings from among the data we found on that level. Thus, the data may be natural but our organization of that data into kinds from which we abstract essences and attach names is our own creation.

The end of Aristotelian thinking meant the end of our access to natural kinds, as we had previously known them, but there was no single solution. We could follow Descartes and create a new way to understand the world through concepts that were clear and distinct, but abstract and nothing like what we actually experience. The other option was to follow Locke and base our ideas of kinds upon the judgments and conventions of past generations that we simply inherit through language acquisition in the hope that in the future we would have access to the real essences that existed on the microscopic level. Of course, on that level we did not even have the conventional essences that language provides from which to begin; so we were on our own in forming the groupings from which to abstract such real essences.

CHAPTER FIVE

A Priori *and* A Posteriori: *David Hume and Immanuel Kant*

The two very different notions of natural kinds that we saw in the last chapter were simply one aspect of a more elementary divide over what knowledge should look like and how we should pursue it in the absence of Aristotle. These two different notions of knowledge go all the way back to Heraclitus and Parmenides, and perhaps they are the result of the previously mentioned different hemispheres of the brain and our preference to lean toward one hemisphere or the other. Whatever is behind these two very different ways of trying to understand the world, in the modern period the divide became ever more evident.

Rationalists like Descartes thought that knowledge should look like mathematics, and particularly geometry. The kinds of ideas we encounter in mathematics and geometry are often termed *a priori* ideas. The term *a priori*, and the contrary term *a posteriori*, are Latin terms that became popular in the early modern period because of a disagreement over how science and knowledge in general should proceed in the absence of Aristotle.

A priori truths are not dependent upon any empirical experience but are true prior to experience. Descartes claimed they were innate truths that we know simply by thinking about them without the aid of empirical experience. They are true because their opposite is impossible, and Descartes considered them certain and saw certainty and truth as synonymous. Knowledge claims that were less than certain were mere opinions to rationalists like Descartes. He envisioned a modern science that would be as certain as geometry, since it would be composed of nothing but clear and distinct ideas.

The empiricists of the modern period saw things very differently. They believed that only *a posteriori* ideas, which emanate from actual experience, tell us about the world. The empiricists argued that there were no innate ideas and all ideas came through experience. The Scottish Philosopher David Hume (1711-1776) is an excellent example of the modern empiricist position. Hume argued that only *a posteriori* ideas were informative and *a priori* ideas were mere tautologies. To Hume, *a priori* truths told us that one idea was either always equal to another idea or never equal to another idea. The truth that all bachelors are unmarried men is simply the comparison between our ideas of bachelors and unmarried men, and in making such a comparison we find them always the same. Likewise, when we compare squares with circles, we find them never the same. Although these clear and distinct ideas are certain, they tell us nothing about the world, but only about the relationship between ideas. To Hume, a priori truths were useful tools in order to create artifacts and technology but they told us nothing about our experience of the world. Clear and distinct ideas are merely clear and distinct but, in order to be true, Hume thought an idea had to find support in empirical evidence.

This presented a problem for Hume. If the path to knowledge was through empirical experience rather than innate ideas, then why are human beings smarter than other animals? If experience were the means to truth and knowledge, then why do we consider human beings more knowledgeable than other animals? If knowledge emanated from sensory experience, then the creatures with the best senses should be the most knowledgeable. Human beings are certainly not equipped better than all other animals in terms of empirical senses. Many animals see, smell, and hear better, and some even have sensory apparatus that we cannot even imagine; why are we considered more intelligent? Descartes had a great answer for this with his idea of innate knowledge. According to Descartes, human beings are smarter than other animals because we have a vast amount of innate ideas that allow us to do things like mathematics and all the technology that comes with that. Of course, Hume could not use that answer and had to come up with another explanation.

One explanation that Hume points to is the fact that language allows us to pass information on to the next generation and we do not have to experience everything anew for ourselves, but in addition to this he points to another factor as well, which he seems to think is even more important. What he points to is the fact that human beings reason through much more complex sequences of cause and effect than other animals, and it was this thinking through cause and effect, which was so highly developed in human beings, that caused our knowledge to surpass that of other animals. As Hume investigated this complex idea of cause and effect, it seemed obvious that it was not an *a priori* idea involving the relationship of ideas; that is, the idea of cause and effect did not come to us by comparing one idea with another. If it was an a posteriori idea, however, it must have come to us through experience. Hence, Hume set out to find the experience that gave us the idea of cause and effect.

In examining it more closely, Hume discovered that it was a complex idea composed of three separate ideas that arise out of three separate experiences. The first experience that contributes to the notion of cause and effect is priority in time. The cause always preceded the effect in our experience, and if we were to experience the temporal order in reverse, it would negate the idea of cause and effect. The second experience that gives rise to the idea of cause and effect is propinquity or nearness in terms of physical proximity. When one thing happens before another but they are not in physical proximity to one another, the idea of cause and effect does not occur to us. When these two experiences occur together, they create another idea but it is the idea of superstition, rather than cause and effect. The idea of cause and effect requires a third experience. What is necessary in order to make our idea of cause and effect more than mere superstition is the experience of a necessary connection between the cause and the effect. Unfortunately, when Hume looked for the experience from which that idea arose, he found nothing in actual experience that would support that idea. He therefore concluded that we get this essential third idea of a necessary connection not from an actual experience, but from the imagination.

When we constantly see one event precede another and they are in physical proximity, the mind creates a habit and connects the two events, but it is an operation of the mind and not an experience. This was an enormous advance in our understanding of the human condition. What Hume had discovered was that our experience was much more complicated than simply recording data as given. The mind was also at work in ways of which we were generally oblivious. Much of what we thought we were experiencing in the world was not out there but in us. Furthermore, what Hume thought was at work within us was the imagination, which added something to what we actually experienced. Of course, this explains why magicians can do what they do, since we see not what is there but what the mind imagines is there. Our mind seems to race ahead and imagine connections within the world that may not actually be there in the world but are rather in us. The mind, in observing two events that are in physical proximity, and with the one event preceding the other in several instances, imagines the previous event to be causally connected to the later. Furthermore, after several experiences of the two events following in the same sequence, the mind imagines that in the next instance when the preceding event occurs, the later event will follow. We imagine that the future will be like the past, but there is nothing in actual experience that assures us of that. Hume refers to this as the fallacy of induction. That we think we can predict the future based upon what we have observed in the past is an idea that originates in imagination rather than actual experience, since we never experience the necessary connection between the cause and the effect.

Hume found a similar situation with other ideas, whose truth he initially thought was determined *a posteriori*, but upon examination found that they too originated out of the imagination rather than experience. One such idea was that of "matter." On this point, he sided with immaterialists like Leibniz and Berkeley. He agreed that the idea of matter had no basis in experience and that the idea originated from the fact that we imagine that something must be the cause of perceptions, which is not a perception itself. Thus, matter, like cause and effect, originates in imagination rather than experience. Hume found this to be the case with other ideas as well. For example, we may have the experience of our minds perceiving ideas or images and even creating them, but we do not have an actual experience of the mind as the thing that houses our ideas. We imagine that our own thoughts must be somewhere, so we imagine the mind as the container that houses those thoughts. The fact that Hume discovered that some of our most basic ideas emanated from the imagination rather than reason or experience should not be shocking to us, since we are in the process of tracing the philosophical imagination in order to see how it has created the modern mind. It was, however, shocking to the Enlightenment thinking of Hume's day.

We refer to the 17th and 18th centuries as the Age of Reason and the Enlightenment. At their base was the idea that we were fast discovering how things really worked. The world was no longer a mystery to behold but a puzzle that we were well on our way to solving. Hume threw a monkey wrench into that whole project. This was not only true in the area of philosophy but in terms of religion as well. Christianity in the eighteenth century was becoming ever more rational in order to compete with the growing popularity of science and its claim that reason and science provided a better basis for human existence than faith. In an attempt to keep pace with Enlightenment science, Christian apologists argued for the reasonableness of Christianity. Hume, however, argued that Christianity was a matter of faith and not reason. Even his ethic was not rational but based upon sentiments in the heart. This kind of opposition to Enlightenment rationality caused many to consider Hume an infidel. His fideism might have been acceptable at other times, but not at the height of the Enlightenment. In fact, upon his death his friends stood guard at his grave for several days to assure that no one would desecrate it. The Enlightenment did not receive Hume's skepticism well, but Immanuel Kant would have a different response to Hume.

The German philosopher, Immanuel Kant (1724-1804) responded to David Hume not as others who simply rejected his skepticism as the work of an infidel, but as one who woke him "from his dogmatic slumber." Philosophy, in its most original form, is always about waking up from a slumber during which we simply accepted inherited prejudices without question. What generally wakes us up is something that does violence to a particular prejudice, but at the same time cannot be dismissed simply because it runs contrary to our understanding. For those without a philosophical imagination, there is no other choice but to dismiss what challenges their inherited prejudices in order to preserve the understanding through which they interpret their experience, and from which they get a great sense of security in believing that they *know* how things work. For those with a philosophical imagination, their response to such data is quite different.

David Hume fueled Kant's philosophical imagination and he set out to solve the crisis in his own thinking created by Hume. Kant agreed with Hume that traditional ideas of *a priori* truths were mere tautologies and real knowledge had to originate in experience. Of course, Hume had shown that some of our most basic ideas did not originate in experience at all. Kant wanted to find a way around this dilemma and he did what philosophers typically do: he re-conceptualized the situation in a way that made the problem go away.

Nicolaus Copernicus (1473–1543), faced a similar problem centuries before. Since the time of the Greco-Egyptian astronomer Ptolemy (90–168 CE) we had understood the irregular orbits of the stars and planets through a complicated system of epicycles that explained why the heavenly bodies moved in such irregular orbits, speeding up at times and slowing down at other times. Ptolemy had given a very accurate way of calculating these movements but he could not tell us why heavenly bodies moved in such irregular ways. Instead of trying to explain why the celestial bodies moved as they did, Copernicus turned the situation around and imagined that it was the earth's movement, which created the appearance of such irregular orbits. Copernicus' idea that the earth was moving in an orbit around the sun instead of the sun revolving around the earth met with enormous opposition, since people believed they saw the sun move and not the earth. Eventually, the Copernican idea of a heliocentric world replaced that of a geocentric world. What was behind the Copernican revolution was what is behind most original philosophical thinking, that is, a change of perspective that allows us to see or conceptualize things differently.

Kant had a similar Copernican revolution. He argued that the reason Hume could not trace certain ideas back to an experience was not because they were the product of the imagination but because they were innate ideas which served as the very conditions for all experience and knowledge. Of course, Descartes had argued that we were in possession of hosts of innate ideas, but Kant had something very different in mind. Kant's innate ideas were not things we could know, like Descartes' innate ideas. Rather Kant's were the *a priori* conditions for human experience and therefore were unknowable in principle.

Philosophers had always believed that something must be in the mind in order to process the incoming data. No one ever really imagined that the mind was purely a *tabula rasa* that simply recorded data as given, but neither had anyone really explored what those conditions were. Of course, Aristotle had his active intellect and Locke offered some ideas of how the mind processed data, but Kant set out to explain what those ideas were that were the conditions for human experience and therefore had to precede all experience. He argued that in order to have the kind of experience that is unique to human beings, we would have to be equipped with certain ideas that were essential to that kind of experience and without which we could not experience the world as we do.

The first two ideas that Kant thought had to be innate and the conditions for all experience both internal and external, were those of time and space. Put in simplest terms, time and space are the innate ideas through which we organize both our inward and outward experiences of the world. According to Kant, we organize our experiences internally into memory through the innate idea of time. We do not record experiences in memory randomly but rather according to temporal sequences. We record one experience as having occurred before, after, or roughly at the same time as another. This is the nature of how we record experience in memory, and Kant reasons that the necessary condition for such a faculty to operate in such a way must be that we possess an innate idea of time that preceded all experience. Later we may come to imagine that time has an external reality connected to the world itself, but that is not our original concept of time. Isaac Newton said that time flows equitably, and in order to substantiate that belief, we connect years to the movement of the earth around the sun and days to the movement of the earth on its axis, but that is time as we have learned to think about it and not time as we initially experience it. Our external experience of the world is always present, but in order to think about an endless number of present moments, we invent some way to mark those present moments into a sequence that we can mathematize. Long before human beings ever had such a notion of counting time, however, we had a deeper, innate notion of time that allowed us to record memories according to temporal sequences.

To explain Kant's innate idea of space is a bit more involved, and it might be helpful to give a brief history of modern concepts of space. Descartes, who was a physicist in addition to his contributions in geometry and philosophy, thought that space was synonymous with matter. Isaac Newton had a problem with that idea, since he imagined that, if space was synonymous with matter, all motion would be local or motion in comparison to local matter. Thus, if we were traveling in space and passed one large piece of matter traveling in one direction and another large piece traveling in the opposite direction, against which one do we measure our motion? Wanting some basis from which to establish an absolute standard of motion, Newton claimed that space was very different from matter. He argued that space was the substance into which God had placed matter. Thus, space was something like an absolute grid against which we could measure and calculate all motion. Leibniz responded to this Newtonian idea and called it blasphemous since it meant that God was guilty of arbitrary action; that is, if God had first created space as a physical entity or substance and then filled it in with matter, what was the reason for God having placed the planets and stars exactly where they were? Even if we argue that everything in the universe had to be in perfect relationship to everything else, God could have moved everything in the universe over one quarter of an inch and it would make no difference in how the universe operated. Thus, there was no reason for God having placed the stars and planets in exactly the places he did, which meant that Newton's idea of space left us with a God who did things randomly. Leibniz instead argued that space was not a thing or substance as Newton had imagined. Rather, according to Leibniz, space was not substantial but relational. God created the world and then space was simply the relationship between the things that God had created. From Leibniz's notion that space was relational rather than substantial, Kant took it to the next step and argued that those spatial relations are in us and that by them we organize our experience of the external world. For Kant, space was the way we organize our external experiences, just as time was the way we organize our internal experiences in memory. When we perceive the external world, we have the mental ability to perceive things in spatial relationship to one another: one thing is to the left of another, and something else is in front or above another thing.

These two innate ideas create what Kant refers to as the phenomenal world or the world as we experience it. Notice that this phenomenal world is not the world as it in itself but the world as we perceive and understand it given the mental hardware that is unique to our species. Kant's idea that the only world we had access to was a phenomenal world shaped by our own minds made early critics claim that there was nothing new in what Kant was presenting, since Berkeley had previously introduced us to the idea of a world that was as we perceive it. Kant argued that he was not talking about idealism, as Berkeley understood it, since Kant claimed that there was a noumenal world of things in and for themselves. Of course, we could never experience that world because we only encounter the world as our minds construct it, and not as it is in and for itself. Thus, Kant's early critics asked why believe that there was a noumenal world of things in and for themselves if we could never experience such a world, but only the phenomenal world as our minds construct it? Kant answers this question in his short refutation of idealism in which he argues that even though we cannot experience the noumenal world, it must exist since in order for time to flow equably, as Newton had said, there must be something outside of ourselves against which we mark the equable flow of time. That thing against which we mark the equable flow of time is the noumenal world claims Kant. If a river flowed equably, that would mean there was a bank to the river against which we could measure its flow as equable. If time is in us and we claim its flow is equable, the noumenal world must serve as the thing against which we measure that flow as equable, just as the riverbank gives us a place from which to measure a river's flow. Many see Kant's refutation of idealism as a weakness in his philosophy. Where Kant is strong and where he enormously affected our thinking for the next two centuries was in convincing us that we bring much more to our experience than we previously had imagined. Indeed, our experience is a composite of data and the understanding through which we interpret those data.

After time and space, Kant introduces a host of other innate ideas that serve as the necessary conditions for knowledge, some of which were the very ideas that Hume could not trace back to experience. Thus, while Hume thought that something like the idea of cause and effect was a psychological habit, Kant claimed it was part of the mental hardware necessary for knowledge. The important point is that both men saw things like the idea of cause and effect as something within us rather than in the world. Whether they saw such ideas as emanating from the imagination or native mental hardware, it was something we brought to our experience rather than something given to us in experience. Of course, both men were working out of a philosophical imagination. Kant's imagination certainly produced an explanation of how human knowledge was possible in a way that was more compatible with Enlightenment thinking than Hume's skepticism. The events of the next two centuries, however, produced a mind more compatible with Hume's notion that at the base of human knowledge is an imagination whose depths we had only begun to explore. Interestingly, Kant himself had a hand in propagating that Humean perspective, as we will see in the next chapter.

CHAPTER SIX

Historicism: Immanuel Kant and G.W.F. Hegel

In trying to overcome David Hume's skepticism, Immanuel Kant brought us to a revolutionary way of understanding our experience as phenomenal. After Kant, we could no longer naively believe that we experience the external world as it is, but instead we came to see our experience of the world as a composite of both data and the understanding through which we interpret the data. That, however, was not Kant's only great insight concerning our human condition for which we have to be grateful. Indeed, there are probably several, but I think the one that deserves mention here is his idea of historicism. Although we seldom connect Kant with the idea of historicism, his essay entitled "Idea of a Universal History from a Cosmopolitan Point of View" is one of the first attempts at a philosophy of history and set the stage for the historicism of the 19th century.

Prior to the Enlightenment, there was no philosophy of history primarily because of the belief that the human condition was somewhat static, the same yesterday, today, and forever. There was a history in terms of a record of events, but Kant introduced the idea that human nature was changing over time. The idea that the human condition might change over time was certainly a modern

77

notion and was probably first suggested even before Kant in the writings of G.B. Vico (1668–1744). Before the eighteenth century, however, the idea of a progressive history seemed unlikely. For one thing, earlier generations did not have enough history to consider and therein detect a pattern or logic at work over time. Furthermore, our history up until the modern period did not seem to be particularly progressive. With the advance of knowledge throughout the seventeenth and eighteenth centuries, however, Kant saw the human condition greatly changed and wondered what produced such an advance.

His explanation begins with Aristotle's understanding that living thing change by being drawn toward certain purposeful ends or *teloi*. Aristotle thought of these ends in terms of happiness. The happiness or purposeful end of an acorn is to become an oak tree. Of course, human beings move toward their ends or happiness rationally rather than simply by instinct or a mechanical nature. In his famous example, Aristotle showed that we do everything because of the rational ends we pursue. Why do we make bridles for horses? His answer is in order to be good cavalrymen. Of course, the Greeks wanted to be good cavalrymen so they would be good at war and therefore other groups would leave them alone and they could live in peace. The reason they would want to live in peace is in order to be happy, but when asked why they wanted to be happy there is no answer except "because". Aristotle claimed that happiness was the ultimate end toward which we direct all of our other instrumental ends like bridle making, being good cavalrymen, or living at peace. Thus, happiness is not an instrumental end that leads to some other higher good, but it is the *summa bonum*, or ultimate good behind all we do.

Aristotle thought that principle ran through all of nature and was what made things move and develop the way they do. Within the rest of nature, this happiness, or purposeful end, is part of being a member of that particular species. With human beings, however, in terms of our rational capacities, nature did not provide us with a specific end but instead, according to Kant, gave us reason and free will in order that we could decide our own happiness. Thus, happiness goes beyond the mechanical structure of our animal existence. Kant says, human beings "shall participate in no other happiness or perfection than that which [they] procure for [themselves] apart from instinct, by [their] own reason."

Thus, unlike other species whose end or happiness is the result of their specific nature, human beings are free to create their own ends and pursue what they conceive to be happiness. Furthermore, their rational capacities have a large effect upon determining their choices. Of course, there are several variables regarding both their freedom and the amount of reason behind their choices. Wealth, education, family, and place of origin all contribute to both our freedom and the rational capacities from which we determine the happiness toward which we move. Kant, however, saw another variable in history itself. If reason and human knowledge were accumulating over time, later generations would have a greater capacity for happiness than earlier generations, because there would be a greater amount of reason or knowledge from which to choose our happiness. Consequently, Kant speculated that our very nature was changing over time, since our purposeful end or happiness was open to change because of the accumulation of knowledge. People in the past had been limited in terms of happiness because of the limits of reason or knowledge, but our expanding rational capacities meant that our capacity for happiness was expanding as well. With greater rational capacities came the promise of overcoming disease and suffering. Perhaps we could even overcome aging or at least slow its progress if we understood it sufficiently. If future generations lived longer and were better able to overcome suffering, it seemed to suggest that they would have a greater capacity for happiness than earlier generations. Additionally, things like flush toilets, indoor plumbing, microwave ovens, cell phones, and a host of other products, have certainly given us an idea of happiness much different from people in the past. Although we might consider many of these things superficial in comparison to true human happiness, the advance of knowledge was allowing us to pursue purposeful ends or forms of happiness unknown to earlier generations.

Kant wanted to know what was at the base of our human nature that makes our rational capacities expand. What he points to as the cause of our expanding rational capacities is our unique dual nature of being both social and unsocial. Kant argued that other animal species are either social or unsocial. With social animals, the degree of their social interaction varies from ants and bees that are highly social to the lesser degrees of social interaction that we find with pack animals and schools of aquatic mammals. Other species tend to be unsocial and live primarily lives of isolation from other members of their species. In the case of other animal species, either their social or unsocial nature is in the interest of their survival. To combine the two instincts in the same species would be a disaster, since they would come together out of their social nature but then they would kill one another out of their unsocial nature. That, however, is exactly how Kant describes human nature. Human beings have a desire to interact with other members of their species because of their social nature, but also end up destroying one another because of their unsocial nature. This looks like a formula for extinction, but Kant thought it is also a formula for the development of reason. Either human beings would become extinct because of their dual nature, or they would develop their rational capacities in order to deal with this contradiction. The early development of reason centered on devising better weapons and means of defense, but as our rational capacities developed, they would eventually lead to civilization and ideas of law and justice as a means of dealing with our dual natures. Other animals can survive in a state of nature acting upon instinct alone but not human beings. Human beings must invent ways to survive amid their conflicting natures and that requires the development of reason.

Kant imagined that this natural antagonism is what is ultimately behind the development of our rational capacities. Our social and unsocial nature causes us to come together and compete for resources. Trade between individuals and wars between groups of individuals increase our rational capacities as we struggle to gain advantage amid this antagonism unique to our species. Our educational system down to the present day continues to reinforce the idea that our rational capacities develop only, or at least develop best, through competition. We also see something like this Kantian thinking in other Enlightenment thinkers like Adam Smith (1723-1790) who believed that a market economy would be most rational since our competing self-interest and greed (our unsocial nature) would stimulate our rational capacities to create better products at cheaper prices.

Of course, this dual nature and our expanding rational capacities could also destroy us by developing ever greater weapons of mass destruction. Kant seemed aware of this and thought it is essential to our survival that we develop higher and higher levels of law and government to keep our expanding rational capacities from destroying us. In fact, over a hundred years after his death, Kant's "Idea of a Universal History from a Cosmopolitan Point of View" was one of the catalysts that served as a blueprint for the proposed League of Nations that followed World War I.

Kant reflected the optimism of the Enlightenment belief that the increase of our rational capacities will eventually solve all of our problems, including what he said is the latest and most pressing problem before the human race. What he saw as this most pressing problem is the question of how to make the lawmakers come under the law. In Kant's day, as in our own, lawmakers often made laws in their own interests, rather than in the interest of society. Plato addressed this in *The Republic* and suggested that only a state governed by a philosopher king would be just, since only a philosopher king would have both the power of a king and the wisdom and the moral commitment of a philosopher to do what was in the interest of justice rather than his own self-interest. Of course, that justice lasts only as long as the philosopher king survives. If the next ruler is not both a king and a philosopher, justice is lost. Because of that, and other reasons, Plato's last book, *The Laws*, suggests that a more permanent solution to the question of a just society would be one universally governed by laws rather than individuals. This was Kant's solution as well, but in his day, he had no idea how to accomplish this. It was one thing to establish laws but quite another thing to get those who make the laws come under those same laws. If a law turned out to be not in the interest of those who made the law, they could simply change it and make another law that was in their interest. Kant saw this problem as the "most difficult of its kind and it is the latest to be solved by the human race." Still, he had an Enlightenment confidence that history would solve this problem because of human beings' ever-expanding rational capacities.

Hegel

Kant's little article on the philosophy of history would have a great effect upon German philosophy over the next century. The antagonism that Kant saw at work within our human nature would inspire the German philosopher G.W.F. Hegel (1770-1831) to develop a full-blown philosophy of history. Hegel began with a problem he found in Kant's *Critique of Pure Reason*. There Kant argued that all we can ever know is the phenomenal world constructed by our innate mental hardware. Recall that the critics of Kant's *Critique* saw that as Berkeley all over again. But Kant argued that his philosophy was nothing like Berkeley's, since he believed there was an actual material world out there apart from our awareness of it. Unfortunately, we could not know that world, but if we could not know it why should we believe it exists? Hegel did not find Kant's "refutation of idealism" compelling. The idea of an unknowable, material world was a problem for Hegel, just as it was for Leibniz, Berkeley, and Hume. There had always been the question of how matter could produce ideas. Hegel's solution was to conceive of Kant's noumenal world as mind itself. In other words, what we are observing as the world is a universal mind whose ideas are emerging and developing just as our own minds develop. Thus, for Hegel, we can know the noumenal world because it is the same kind of spiritual substance as our own minds. Furthermore, Hegel's solution to Kant's problem of not being able to know the noumenal world also addressed the problem created by Descartes' dualism. Descartes had claimed that there were two very different kinds of substances: mind and matter. This created the huge problem of trying to explain how those two very different kinds of things interacted. Many modern thinkers became reductionists and tried to overcome Descartes' dualism by reducing everything to either mind or matter. Either everything was reducible to matter and the mind was really just a physical brain, or the only things that existed were minds and the ideas they produce (e.g., Leibniz and Berkeley). Hegel took the idealist position a step further than Leibniz and Berkeley by claiming that the world itself was mind. Furthermore, all the innate ideas that Kant thought were part of our individual mind's hardware, Hegel argued were part of the world's mind as well. Not only is the world itself a mind but it develops much in the same way that our individual minds develop. Hegel argued that the same antagonism we find at work in our individual lives is replicated in the history of the world itself, and just as that antagonism causes our individual minds to develop, it causes the world's mind to develop as well. Just as someone might write a biography or memoir of the development of one's own mind, Hegel writes about how the world's mind has developed.

Like Kant, Hegel sees an antagonism at work in history that causes the mind that is the world to develop. Unlike Kant's antagonism of our "unsocial/sociability," however, Hegel sees myriads of triads at work within history whereby we try to conceptualize a situation in a certain way, but when that proves less than fruitful, our response is to take the opposite approach, again to no avail. The situation is resolved when we find a way to bring these two opposing views together. Hegel takes us through example after example of how the mind that is at work within the world resolves these conflicting perspectives. We have been seeing something very similar throughout this book. Heraclitus found that his way of conceptualizing the world left us without the possibility of knowledge; Parmenides took us in a different direction into the abstract world of mathematics. Plato tried to synthesis these two into a perspective he articulated with things like the cave allegory or simile of the line. Plato's failure to provide a way to the otherworld forms, however, caused Aristotle to move in a completely different direction. However, the discovery of the microscopic world ended the Aristotelian perspective and a completely new way to conceptualize the world was necessary. While Descartes suggested we proceed in one direction, Locke and Hume suggested another. Kant eventually resolved that conflict but created another that Hegel tried to resolve.

What Hegel had come to discover was that the mind, be it our own individual mind or the mind that is unfolding throughout history, is forever assuming new perspectives in order to make sense of our human experience. We constantly face circumstances that convince the rational element within us that our present perspective is inadequate to make sense of what is before us. Of course, there is always resistance to a change of perspective since the belief that our perspectives represent truth itself offers a great sense of security, albeit a false one. In spite of opposition from the status quo, history always wins and we adapt to a perspective that makes more sense of our experience.

Of course, Hegel's particular picture of history leaves us with much to question, but his great contribution to the modern mind comes more from his logic than his particular picture of history. The logic he describes is very different from the logic that had dominated thinking in the West since the time of Aristotle, but it was not completely new either. Indeed, since the time of the Platonic dialogues, we had been aware of a dialectical logic that moved from thesis to antithesis, and then synthesis. Furthermore, Kant had used a dialectical logic in his explanation of history, but Hegel would delve deeper into that logic and its connection to human reason.

To understand Hegel's logic, however, we need first to consider the logic that had been so dominant in Western thinking in order to see how different Hegel's logic was. Since the time of Plato and Aristotle, Western logic found its basis in what were termed, "the laws of thought." These laws included the law of identity ($A = A$), the law of non-contradiction (A does not equal ~A), and the law of excluded middle (Either A or ~A but not both A and ~A). We can actually trace the law of non-contradiction to Parmenides, but it was Plato and Aristotle who put that law into a context that would not lead to absurd conclusions. Plato knew that the law of non-contradiction was absurd unless it was restricted. In the *Euthydemus*, Euthydemus' brother Dionysodorus argues that the interlocutor, Clinias, must be the father of a dog, since the dog had a father, and Clinias has admitted that he is a father (298d-299). Since by the law of non-contradiction, one cannot both be a father and not be a father at the same time, Clinias must be the father of the dog. Although Clinias is obviously not the father of the dog, it was not so obvious in Plato's day where Dionysidorus' thinking went wrong. Thus, Plato attempted to sort out where and when the law of non-contradiction applies and where and when it does not apply.

The restriction that Plato places on the law of non-contradiction is that it must be "in the same respect," and "at the same time." Thus, Plato attempts to isolate the object of thought by removing it from all other time but the present and from all respects but one. Although we are involved in many relationships, when we think about ourselves relationally, we must restrict our thinking to one relationship at one time in order for the law of non-contradiction to be applicable in a way that does not lead to absurd conclusions.

Like Plato, Aristotle also believed that the law of non-contradiction (along with the law of identity and the law of excluded middle) was the cornerstone of all right thinking, but it had to be restricted. What he says is little different from Plato; that is, he shows where they are appropriate and where they are not.[5] They are appropriate only when applied to attributes and to attributes at a particular time and in a particular respect. "The same attribute cannot at the same time belong and not belong to the same subject and in the same respect."[6]

By limiting the law of non-contradiction in this way, Aristotle overcame Heraclitus' claim that identity contains contradictions because the attributes of a thing change over time. By isolating identity in one moment of time, Aristotle abstracts the objects of thought just as Plato had done. Thus, identity is set in a different light than it had been for Heraclitus who understood

---

5. See, Metaphysics G, 3&4; De Interpretatione 11, 21a32-33; Topics IV 1, 121a22-4; Sophistical Refutations 5, 167a1-6.

6. Metaphysics G, 3,1005b18-20.

identity as dynamic and thus involving change and contradictions. For both Plato and Aristotle, identity is an abstraction in that we must abstract whatever we focus our thinking upon from time and all circumstances but one. Thus, these laws of identity, non-contradiction, and excluded middle, which we have dubbed the "laws of thought," are in reality laws of analysis; that is, in order for them to work we must analyze something into smaller and smaller units until the contradictions all disappear. Such analytic thinking has dominated the Western mind since the time of Plato and Aristotle and became especially dominant in the modern era.

What Hegel introduced with his logic are the laws that govern synthetic thinking. We are not simply left-brained, analytic thinkers but are capable of thinking synthetically as well. When we do think synthetically and put things together in order to find patterns within our experience, we must bear contradictions and tolerate ideas that are often vague and ambiguous. Hegel claims that the law of identity that governs synthetic thinking is that A equals not A ($A = \sim A$). In other words, to understand A in a larger and more comprehensive context we must also understand what A is not. To say that $A = A$ is a tautology and has little meaning. It tells us nothing about A, other than A is A. The only way a thing truly takes on identity is through what it is not or, in Hegel's terms, through its otherness. What a thing is not is necessary to the identity of a thing, because what it is not is what gives boundaries, definition, and meaning to a thing. Thus, its otherness must be contained within the very identity of the thing.

Hegel also attacks the law of non-contradiction and shows it to be merely one mode of thought, rather than being synonymous with rational thought itself. In a very interesting passage, he says something that appears shocking to those who strictly adhere to the traditional laws of thought and imagine that analytic thinking is the only form of right thinking. He says, "Something moves, not because at one moment it is here and at another there, but because at one and the same moment it is here and not here, because in this 'here', it at once is and is not."[7]

This is an obvious contradiction, and the traditional laws of thought would say that it is impossible for something to be here and not here at the same time. Of course, what is behind Hegel's statement is the matter of how we conceive of time. If we think of things like time or motion analytically, and the continuum on which they exist moves from one fixed, analyzable point to another (i.e., t_1, t_2, t_3 . . .), thus constituting a series of present moments where something is here and nowhere else, then Hegel is certainly wrong. If that is the case, then something is here (e.g., t_4) and not any place else. If, however, there are no fixed points on the continuum that is time, and time is continually moving, like motion, then we cannot stop and analyze time without making it something other than what it is. If the nature of time, like motion, defies arrest, then Hegel is right and analytic thinking is not suited to understand such things as time or motion. To think of time as an ongoing continuum forces us to think contrary to the laws of non-contradiction and excluded middle, and to understand that something is both here and not here at the same moment.

If motion defies the traditional laws of thought, then all living things violate the laws of thought as well, since they are in constant motion, not in the sense that they experience constant local

---

7. Hegel G.W.F. *Science of Logic*. Trans. A. V. Miller. (New York: Humanities Press, 1969). 440.

motion but in the sense that all living things experience perpetual internal motion. This internal motion of all living things prevents them from having any fixed, analyzable point of identity. Here Hegel says, "Abstract self-identity is not as yet a livingness.... Something is therefore alive only in so far as it contains contradictions within it."[8]

Hegel's logic is synthetic and joins things into ever-greater wholes rather than analyzing them into ever-smaller parts. Thus, the traditional laws of thought are not the laws that govern all of reason, but only abstract, analytical reason. As we have seen, the way analytical reason eliminates contradictions is by dividing things into ever-smaller elements until the contradictions disappear. When Plato and Aristotle qualify the law of non-contradiction and say "in the same respect," and "at the same time," what they are doing is breaking a thing down into frozen elements. We are no longer talking about Socrates but one particular aspect of Socrates at one particular time. If we focus on one particular aspect of a thing, at one particular time, the laws of non-contradiction and excluded middle work. When, however, we deal with the whole, rather than the particular aspects of a thing, we are treating all the respects and times together and then we certainly encounter contradictions and the truth is often both/and rather than either/or. When we say that life is full of joy and sorrow, we can eliminate that contradiction, or any such contradiction, by analyzing life and dividing it into joyous parts and sorrowful parts. That is, in one respect, it is joyous and in another respect, it is sorrowful.

---

8. Hegel, G.W.F. *The Logic of Hegel*. Trans. Willian Wallace. *The Encyclopedia of the Philosophical Sciences*. (New York: Oxford University Press, 1972). 75.

If, however, we leave life (or anything) whole and do not analyze it into this respect or that respect, we see myriads of contradictions. Our modern culture has taught us to think analytically about abstracted parts of our experience so that the traditional laws of thought work and give us clear and distinct ideas. This kind of myopic reasoning is certainly valuable and aids us in many ways, but it should not be our only form of reason.

What Hegel offers is a logic that stands back and looks at history from a distance in order to see, amid the contradictions and ambiguities, a pattern. Thus, Hegel's famous line, "the truth is the whole." Indeed, when we examine history as a whole, we see patterns at work that unfold through what Hegel describes as triads. Although Hegel never uses the terms thesis, antithesis, and synthesis, which we associate with the logic of a dialogue, something like that is certainly going on with Hegel's triads. So much of our history seems to be a matter of our trying to create a perspectival understanding that will account for our experience, only to find problems with that perspective that eventually lead to another perspective, which seems a better way to explain and make sense of what is before us. The human mind is constantly changing in order to makes sense of our experience. Historicism is the term we use to express this process and the evolving mind it creates.

Hegel's philosophical imagination provided two great contributions to the evolution of the modern mind. One was the idea of a synthetic logic by which we could know not simply by analyzing things into ever-smaller parts until the contradictions all disappear, but by putting things together in order to see patterns that are not accessible to analytic thinking. Hegel's other great contribution was historicism and the fact that the human mind changes over time. Both ideas presented major challenges to modernity and the Enlightenment project, but that is part of the evolutionary nature of the human mind and the great challenge to the philosophical imagination.

CHAPTER SEVEN

Existentialism:
Albert Camus and Soren Kierkegaard

The philosophical imagination is always trying to provide a way to make sense of our experience. From earlier generations, we inherit our initial philosophical perspectives or way of seeing and making sense of the world, and as long as that perspective continues to make sense, we go about our lives as if we know what is going on. An existential crisis arises when those perspectives fail to make sense of our experience. Of course, this is what we have been observing by considering the history of modern philosophy, but not all such crises are existential crises. A crisis concerning our perspective might concern only a minor aspect of our life, for example, when our way of going about a particular thing no longer seems to be productive and there is a need to change the way we understand what we are doing. It could even be something that changes the way we see the world, but that change does not affect our core beliefs or the perspective from which we draw meaning. Copernicus's revolutionary notion of a heliocentric universe certainly changed the way many people saw the world, but for most it did not result in an existential crisis. For others, however, who believed that God had given us sufficient knowledge of all that we needed to know, it may have threatened a sacred part of their

93

perspective, but still that might not amount to an existential crisis, since it may be easy for some simply to dismiss the threatening new view of the world as nonsense. What causes an existential crisis is new data that threatens to destroy the old perspective, but, at the same time, we can neither deny nor dismiss the data.

Although human beings have always experienced existential crises from time to time, we have only begun to talk about these experiences in existential terms over the last two centuries. Similarly, human beings have always had an unconscious but were unaware of it until Freud; likewise, an evolutionary process whereby species change over time had always been going on in spite of the fact that we were largely unaware of the details of that process until Darwin. The same was true of the existential crisis. Certainly, the plague known as the Black Death in the fourteenth century produced existential crises in many people, as did the potato famine in Ireland in the nineteenth century, although people were without existential terms to express the experience at that time. In fact, it only became popular to interpret such an experience in existential terms after World War II.

The French philosophers Jean-Paul Sartre (1905–1980) and Albert Camus (1913–1960) articulated, in existential terms, what many people had experienced during the war. The experience they were trying to express was that of having whatever it was that provided meaning taken from them and finding themselves left with mere existence. Prior to the war, life may have made sense because of beliefs in religion, morality, humanity, or science. Others had found meaning in the love they experienced in families or the kindness that existed among neighbors, but the unexpected loss of those loved ones because of unthinkable evil

Existentialism: Albert Camus and Soren Kierkegaard

and suffering of a world war caused many to fall into an existential despair.

As we have seen, the philosophical imagination is always trying to create a perspective that will explain and make sense of what is before us. The enormous carnage and barbarism of a world at war destroyed many of those previously held perspectives, and large numbers of people found themselves with nothing to cling to but existence. Thus, the existential question became, "How are we to live with existence alone and without what had previously given us hope for a meaningful existence?"

This is yet another example of our inherited understanding of the world no longer making sense, and the need for the philosophical imagination to create a new way to perceive and make sense of our existence. For existentialists like Sartre and Camus, what was ultimately before them was the *absurd*. The absurd is the word that existentialists use to describe the ultimate reality of the human condition. We may pretend that life is meaningful and ignore the reality of death by becoming involved in all the petty things in which we desperately try to find meaning, but the war put death on center stage where it was hard to ignore. What could possibly be the meaning of life when it ultimately ends in meaningless death? In normal times we can keep death at enough of a distance to imagine that it will never happen to us, but the war brought death home to so many who had lost loved ones at such a young and unexpected age that it could no longer be ignored. Death was the main story of the war and demanded our attention.

Of course, there had always been similar situations in history but what made a world war in the twentieth century unique was that it followed an Enlightenment that promised that such things were behind us. We were no longer barbarians, but had elevated our human condition to new heights. Barbarism in the past was to be expected, but in the twentieth century it came as a shock that demanded an explanation. We thought we had ascended to such great heights only to see that come crashing down. World War I, a minor European conflict by comparison to World War II, was termed the "war to end all wars," only to be followed a generation later by a war that engulfed the entire world. What happened to the enlightened advance of reason?

Albert Camus articulates what he sees as the human condition in light of World War II with the *Myth of Sisyphus*. In Greek mythology, Sisyphus is condemned for a crime against the gods, to roll a huge stone to the top of a mountain only to have it roll back down again. Sisyphus must repeat this labor every day for eternity. This is an interesting hell and one that Camus thinks portrays the human condition. In rolling our rock to the top of the hill, it appears that our lives have purpose and we are accomplishing something and getting somewhere. But that is an illusion since the rock always rolls back down the hill again. We imagined that Enlightenment science was getting us somewhere, but the war revealed that as the illusion of Sisyphus getting his rock to the top of the hill. All of our efforts end in death, which makes all of our struggles meaningless. Camus imagines that the Sisyphus myth best describes our human condition as both individuals and as a species. We extend great effort to get our rock to the top of the hill, thinking that doing so is somehow meaningful, but with our death the rock rolls back down the hill and nothing is really accomplished.

The great ambition of the Enlightenment was to advance civilization by our rational efforts, but World War II revealed that such ambition came to the same end as the Sisyphus myth. Reason had produced only a more efficient barbarism and death on a scale previously unimaginable. Faced with this reality, how do we create a perspective that can provide meaning in such a meaningless existence? Camus' solution to this existential dilemma was rebellion, simply because that is what the best and bravest among us do. It is a unique form of rebellion, however, since it is without hope of ever changing the reality of the absurd. Other rebellions have an aim, purpose, or something to accomplish and therein end the rebellion, but there is no end to Camus' existential rebellion, since existential rebels cannot change the situation against which they rebel. The purpose of Camus' rebellion is merely to remain conscious of the truth of the absurd. Only by means of rebellion can one truly face up to the meaninglessness of life. If we simply accept life as absurd, we will find that as much as we profess that belief, we will very quickly begin to act as if life does have meaning. We will ignore our own impending death and everyone else's death and pretend that getting this rock to the top of the hill really matters. The other alternative is no better; to commit suicide in despair over the absurd is also to let it fall from consciousness and thereby turn from its truth. Camus thought that the only way to face the truth of the absurd is by making it the object of our rebellion. The best and bravest among us, he said, are willing to face reality as it is, without the aid of imagined beliefs that attempt to make sense of an absurd existence.

Of course, most people do not want to live in the midst of an existential crisis, and instead of facing the absurd, they cling to the little stories they received at their mother's knee about religion, morality, or family. They tell themselves freedom or love or some other noble virtue makes life meaningful. They find others who have the same trust in a similar story and spend time in their company in order to make their little story appear to be *the* story that everyone they know believes. If they find the group's story becomes different from their own, they leave that group and go in search of another group that does endorse their story. We somehow trust these little stories and somehow extract a sense of security from them by imagining them to represent something more than the petty way we try to create meaning for our lives. The existentialist, however, is one who rejects those little stories and is willing to face and embrace the fact that a life of suffering that always ends in death is an absurdity that no little story can mitigate.

Kierkegaard

Although the French existentialists of the twentieth century popularized existentialism and brought it to the attention of the masses, existentialism actually had its origin in the nineteenth century with the Danish philosopher, Soren Kierkegaard (1813-1855). Like the French existentialists of the twentieth century, Kierkegaard's existentialism amounted to a rejection of the perspective and understanding that was supposed to provide his life with meaning. The circumstance of Kierkegaard's existential crisis, however, was very different from that of someone like Camus. Kierkegaard's existential crisis resulted from a religious experience he had during Easter week of 1848. Kierkegaard could not deny the experience, but it was considerably out of step with the common notion of Christianity of his day. Kierkegaard chose to trust his experience and allow it to destroy his inherited understanding. Of course, many historical figures have had religious experiences that caused them to reject their previously held perspective. Augustine, Francis Assisi, and Martin Luther could not deny their religious experiences and therefore had to reform their understanding to accommodate their experience, but Kierkegaard's experience led to a uniquely existential response.

At the base of his experience was the revelation that God had forgiven all of his sins and he was at one with God. That was very different from what Christian theology had led him to believe. The Christian theologies of the period gave formulas whereby God forgives sins, but Kierkegaard's experience seems to have bypassed those formulas and had nothing to do with his believing or doing anything. Christian doctrine had always maintained that Jesus atoned for our sins on the cross, but there were things we had to do or believe in order to receive that forgiveness. Sacraments or professions of faith were required in order to give us access to God's forgiveness, and then right moral action was required to maintain that forgiveness. Christian theology in almost all of its forms insisted that such forgiveness and mercy were conditional and required some action or belief on our part. What Kierkegaard experienced, however, was a forgiveness that required nothing from us but that we accept our need for forgiveness and mercy.

Before that experience, Kierkegaard considered himself a Christian, as did nearly everyone in nineteenth century Denmark. After that experience, however, he no longer thought of himself as a Christian. The problem was that his experience was radically different from what everyone else in Denmark held to be Christianity. Thus, Kierkegaard's crisis was one of either clinging to what everyone else believed and taking confidence in the belief that millions of people could not be wrong, or trusting his own experience. Kierkegaard's decision was to trust the latter, and the rest of his life centered on writing about this subjective truth and the angst that people experience when they decide to pursue the truth of their own experience rather than the conventional truths that provide a sense of meaning for so many.

Just as World War II destroyed many people's conventional beliefs, Kierkegaard's religious experience destroyed the religious beliefs that so many others saw as sacred. Once the conventional truths in which others find meaning and security are gone, we must find meaning on our own. This is a major theme which underlies all forms of existentialism. In spite of this universal characteristic of the existential experience, Kierkegaard's existentialism is unique and very different from that of a twentieth century existentialist like Camus. Camus, for instance, thought that life was absurd because it was meaningless, since all the little stories we make up in order to make sense of life and death are absurd in the light of the massive evil, suffering, and death brought about by a world war. Kierkegaard, on the other hand, saw the Christianity of his day as absurd in light of his religious experience.

In order to understand Kierkegaard's unique notion of the absurd, we have to see it in contrast to the dominant notion of Christianity of his day, which had become progressively more rational throughout the modern period. Perhaps in order to keep pace with the growing popularity of modern science and the Enlightenment, modern Christianity insisted that its beliefs and doctrines had a basis in reason. For example, by the eighteenth century, many Christians considered David Hume an atheist, not because he did not believe in God, but because he thought that religious faith was not rational and was a matter exclusively of faith.

Hume's fideism was out of step with modern Christianity, since what had become sacred to Christianity was not faith, but a faith founded upon reason. By the nineteenth century, the modern mind had become so rational that some even argued that it was immoral for anyone to hold beliefs that they could not support with either empirical evidence or reason. Kierkegaard was certainly an anathema to such rational people, but those who were most upset with Kierkegaard were the religious people who wanted a reward for their righteous beliefs and good moral behavior. The idea of a God who extends mercy without restriction is troubling to good people who want a just God who rewards goodness and punishes evil. Kierkegaard's idea of a God who extends mercy without restriction is troubling to many religious types who want a God who is more like us—a God who judges according to our ideas of good and evil, and responds as we would. So religious people devise theological formulas that will allow some to be worthy of forgiveness and mercy, but not others. This is certainly rational and in keeping with everything we know about how the world works and how morality and justice works. Theological judgement is compatible with all of our most sacred prejudices, but that is exactly what Kierkegaard's revelation seemed to destroy.

Thus, like Camus, Kierkegaard faced the absurd. The absurd for Kierkegaard, however, was twofold. For Camus, the War revealed how meaningless and absurd life was. Camus' reaction to the reality of the absurd was rebellion, which he thought was not absurd but was a reasonable and courageous response to the absurd. For Kierkegaard, on the other hand, not only was the Christian theology of his day absurd in the light of his religious experience, but his solution to his existential crisis was absurd as well.

Having lost the Christian theology that had been his inherited understanding, Kierkegaard turned to the Gospel itself. What he found there was something even more absurd than Christian theology. Seeing the Gospel as absurd was not an entirely new idea. The second century Christian, Tertullian (160–220 AD), was the first to have said, "Credo quia absurdum est" (I believe because it is absurd), but Kierkegaard developed this idea into a Christian existentialism. Although he had little influence in his own day, Kierkegaard would have an enormous influence upon twentieth century philosophy and theology.

The idea that the Gospel was absurd and that was its actual evidence certainly appears strange, especially to our modern minds, but there is at least the hint of absurdist reasoning in the Jewish canon. In the books of Job and Ecclesiastes, we see the absurdity of suffering (Job) and the absurdity of pleasure (Ecclesiastes). Human beings have forever searched for an explanation for evil and suffering. The theological question is: Why, if God is omnificent, omnibenevolent, omnipotent, and omniscient, is there evil and suffering in the world? This is the question that Job asks of God and receives no answer other than God's ways are not our ways. In the other absurdist book (Ecclesiastes), we find the absurdity of pleasure. The writer of Ecclesiastes tells us that he gave himself to every pleasure and found it all meaningless. We live lives seeking pleasure and trying to avoid pain and suffering, but have no idea what it all means.

What Kierkegaard saw in the Gospels was not answers to this question but a deeper revelation of the absurd. What Kierkegaard saw in the Gospels was a story about the God who created this world of enormous evil and suffering, assumed a human form, and entered into that world in order to suffer and die on a Roman cross. That is certainly absurd, but it is what Kierkegaard and Tertullian before him found so appealing about the Gospels. Kierkegaard thought that the great evidence for the truth of the Gospels was that they defy human imagination, because they are not the product of human imagination.

The philosophical imagination that we have been tracing throughout this book is about coming up with a story that makes sense of what is before us, when what is before us does not make sense. The Gospels, however, do not make sense of what we experience, but instead confound us and reduce us to a state of not knowing. Everything about the Gospels seems absurd and out of touch with what human beings consider rational. The idea of an infinite God becoming a finite human being is certainly absurd. How does the infinite become the finite? How can one be both a man and God? Of course, the Romans had emperors who were gods, but they were human gods. They thought like us and valued what we valued. Those gods did not tell us to do good to those that hate us. They did not tell us to bless those that curse us and pray for those who mistreat us. They did not tell us that if someone slaps you on one cheek, to turn to them the other cheek and let them slap you again. They never told us that if someone takes your coat, give him your shirt as well, and that we should give to all who ask, and if anyone takes what belongs to you, do not demand it back. They never told us to love our enemies, and do good to them in order that we would be like this absurd God who was kind to the ungrateful and wicked.[9]

---

9. Luke 6:27-36.

So much of what Jesus says and does is absurd. He tells us that the last will be first and the first will be last,[10] and that there is more rejoicing in heaven over one sinner who repents than over ninety-nine righteous people that have no need of repentance.[11] In the parable about the prodigal, he tells us about two sons. One does it right and that turns out to be bad, and another who does it wrong and that turns out to be good. Jesus prays for his torturers to receive forgiveness, which is absurd, but whenever someone takes Jesus seriously and does likewise, we stand in awe because we recognize we are in the presence of something divine. To Kierkegaard, Jesus turned the world upside down and told us that we are wrong about almost everything.

Kierkegaard saw Jesus as revealing a divinity that is far beyond our comprehension. Because of this, Kierkegaard saw true followers of Jesus as not seeking a rational truth that makes sense to our human way of thinking and knowing. For Kierkegaard, faith aspires to a different type of truth. It is a subjective truth that is personal and involves a different type of knowing than the dominant notion that became so popular in the modern era. That way of thinking had produced theologies that stressed the universal and objective nature of faith, which was very much in keeping with the mood of the modern era. The existential faith that Kierkegaard describes begins with the realization that spiritual experience is very different from other forms of human experience. Faith, or at least existential faith, is the willingness to go against the common notion because of an experience which the individual cannot deny or dismiss, in spite of the fact that it does not conform to

---

10. Matt. 20:16.
11. Luke 15:7.

common understanding. Jesus' initial followers followed him and rejected the common understanding not because what Jesus said made sense, but because of the experience of his presence, which they could neither deny nor fully understand.

What Kierkegaard attacked is the modern idea of religious faith as a trust in a theology or a certain conceptual understanding, rather than a faith in a man whom Christians regard as divine. We have seen throughout this text that our understanding of the world is always traceable back to the philosophical imagination through which we interpret our experience. Our tendency is to think that whatever philosophical perspective or conceptual understanding we accept for ourselves is *the* true perspective and the one that all right-thinking people should embrace. That shows a lack of understanding of history and, in particular, a lack of understanding of how the human perspective has evolved over time. Our tendency to think of our perspective as some objective truth also shows a lack of understanding of what Jesus said and did, since those things, if taken seriously will do violence to whatever one's perspective might be. What Kierkegaard suggests is to allow what Jesus said and did to create a subjective truth or, as he says, "A truth for which I might live or die." This idea of a personal or subjective truth is reminiscent of the medieval mystical tradition. Mysticism was personal, while modern Christianity had become objective and universal in spite of the fact that it continued to splinter into thousands of different denominations, each claiming to have the objective and universal truth. Kierkegaard's great contribution was to reveal how personal and subjective our experience, especially spiritual experience, really is, and that such experience cannot be interpreted through our inherited conceptual understanding that is provided by our culture, history, and language community.

Of course, the vast majority of people resist the existential experience of which Kierkegaard speaks and cling to their inherited conceptual understand of God and the world. Many see any break from that conventional understanding as a sign of insanity. Indeed, to see the world differently than everyone else is what many take to be the definition of insanity; so this existential move away from the conventional understanding, in which everyone else trusts and finds security, is a frightening move for the individual. It produces angst within the individual, but it is also what has fueled the evolution of the modern mind.

In Kierkegaard's case, he seemed to find comfort in the fact that what Jesus said and did supported his own spiritual experiences and he attempted to build an understanding around those things rather than accept the Christianity of his day. Of course, that put him at odds with the socio-cultural world of nineteenth century Denmark, but by so doing, Kierkegaard gave later existentialists a model to help them negotiate their existential crises. By trusting his own experience rather than the ideologies, prejudices, and values that he had inherited from the conventions and judgments of past generations, Kierkegaard provided another great example of that unique form of philosophical intelligence that has produced civilization and the evolution of human consciousness. It is, however, the least practiced and most rare form of human intelligence since it requires the courage to stand alone and trust one's experience rather than the conventions that purport to make sense of our experience.

CHAPTER EIGHT

Pragmatism: William James

In the last chapter we spoke of Kierkegaard's concept of "subjective truth." Many people have trouble with that and think that a subjective truth is no truth at all. Most people conceive of truth as objective, universal, and even obvious. I often hear people say, "The truth is the truth," but truth is actually a difficult concept, and there are different theories concerning it. According to the oldest of these theories, a statement or belief is true if it corresponds to observable facts. The proposition "the grass is green" is true if it corresponds to the fact that the particular grass in question is indeed green. Such a theory works well on propositions about physical states of affairs and is the basis for experiments. We can test to see if a statement about an actual state of affairs is true by reproducing it in an experiment. Likewise, in many other areas of life we try to determine the truth about statements by finding whether or not they correspond to facts.

The problem with the correspondence theory is that not all propositions are about a particular physical state of affairs that can be either verified or falsified. This is especially true of philosophical matters since they are seldom about a physical state of affairs, but rather about how we conceptualize and think about things. When we make statements about how we think about things there are no external data to confirm our propositions. If the mind was purely a *tabula rasa* and nothing was in our head but ideas that were traceable to an actual experience, perhaps a correspondence theory would suffice. Since, however, activities like mathematics and philosophy are about the way we think about things rather than facts about the world, correspondence theory cannot help to get us at the truth of such matters. Furthermore, what history has been progressively revealing is that a great deal of what we experience is the result of what is in us rather than in the world. Since the time of Kant, we have known that the only world to which we have access is a phenomenal world, which is a composite of the world's data and the perspectives through which we interpret that data.

Furthermore, the last two centuries have convinced us that we bring much more to the data of our experience than Kant's innate mental hardware. We now know that in addition to whatever innate mental hardware we may possess, we also interpret the data of our experience through perspectives that are historical, cultural, linguistic, and philosophical. Thus, by what criterion are we to judge the truth of that part of our phenomenal experience that we bring to the data? Such things are in us and not out there in the world and therefore cannot be verified or falsified by observation. Recall the previously mentioned logical positivists of the twentieth century who claimed that only statements about actual physical states of affairs were meaningful; such a claim, however, was not meaningful by its own criterion. The problem with the correspondence theory is that it leaves us with a very truncated notion of truth that does not allow us to get beyond the idea of truth as fact.

Of course, Hegel gave us a way to preserve a correspondence theory of truth by claiming that the world itself was mind and therefore we could claim our theories are true when they correspond to the theories that are unfolding throughout history. People with unpopular theories often believe that history will exonerate them. Only the future will tell us which theories history exonerates and which were simply mistaken. Until then, such correspondence is not something we can employ in order to know the truth of our theories; so another theory is necessary. That other theory of truth is the coherence theory.

A coherence theory of truth claims that something is true if it makes sense or is internally coherent. A coherence approach to truth is better able to deal with theories since it judges something as true when it gives us a coherent picture or story that makes sense. Mathematics is true by coherence and rationalist philosophers are attracted to coherence because of a belief that we best pursue truth through reason rather than experience. Some point to Descartes as an example of such a theory since he used the examples of mathematics and geometry to pursue truth: mathematics and geometry are true not because they correspond to observable reality but because they are internally consistent or coherent. There are no twos or sevens in the world of our experience. Likewise, there are no circles or triangles. A circle is a figure in which every point is equidistant from the center. No matter how carefully we draw and try to replicate that in actual experience it is never exactly a circle. That is why a circle is an abstract idea and, at least for people like Pythagoras, Parmenides, and Plato, represented a higher level of reality because it was an eternal and immutable idea unlike the ideas that emanate from our experience of the world.

Not only are mathematical and geometric concepts immutable and eternal in comparison to the objects of our experience, but mathematical systems are enormously coherent with very few anomalies or inconsistencies.[12] Because of that, human beings have long thought that it would be ideal to have an understanding of the world modelled after mathematics. Recall that one of the major attractions of corpuscular philosophy was that it offered the possibility of a mathematical physics. Thus, the idea that something is true because of its internal coherence is certainly an appealing way to think about truth, especially the truth of our beliefs and theories, which we cannot verify by their correspondence to actual states of affairs.

Of course, coherence theories, when they are about actual physical states of affairs, rather than the purely abstract realm of mathematics also have to *save the appearance*, or give an account of what we actually experience. At first, this did not seem to be enough to establish a belief as *true*, but as our understanding of the human condition progressed, it became evermore apparent that it might be the best we could achieve. Initially, late medieval or early modern thinking did not see coherence as a way to truth but merely a way to save the appearance. When Galileo started teaching Copernicus's theory of a heliocentric rather than geocentric universe, the church told him he could teach it as *saving the appearance* but not as truth, since Ptolemy's theory of a geocentric universe also saved the appearance or explained what we were seeing.

The church thought that truth had to be more than merely some way to account for what we were seeing, since multiple

---

12. One such anomaly is the fact that $1/3$, plus $1/3$, plus $1/3 = 1$; but $.3333.....$, plus $.3333.....$, plus $.3333.....$, equals $.9999......$

theories could do that. Of course, Galileo thought that Copernicus saved the appearance much better than Ptolemy did, and for that reason, his theory was *true*. In time, we would come to recognize the coherence theory of truth as legitimate, although what always plagues that theory is the fact that multiple theories can save the appearance. Several years ago, two economists with conflicting theories split the Noble Prize for economics. Both theories were coherent and saved the appearance but could they both be true? Are there possibly multiple ways to make sense of our world? The famous Copenhagen decision where scientists came to agree that sometimes light appears to be of a wave nature and sometimes a corpuscular nature is a case in point, as are the multiple personality theories in psychology, which all appear coherent and explanatory. Perhaps the greatest example of this problem with coherence is in theology where people read the same sacred text and come up with innumerable coherent theories concerning the truth and meaning of that text.

Coherence may not get us to an ideal notion of truth but, given our human condition, it is often the best we can do. We employ it constantly in order to judge whether someone is lying. If we cannot get at the facts to either verify or falsify their story, rather than concede and claim we have no way of knowing whether their account is true or not, we make judgments based upon how coherent the story is. Of course, if we are able to verify or falsify the details of the story by observation, or reproduce the details in an experiment, we can do that, but often we do not have access to the experience or cannot reproduce it in an experiment, and thus must rely on how coherent the story is. This is often the case in courts of law where we do not always have access to facts but must rely on the testimony of people and we must judge the truth of those testimonies on a basis of how coherent and consistent they are with what we know about human nature and the nature of the world. Of course, the fact that one account appears more coherent than another does not mean that that one is true and the other not true. It could simply be that one person explains or presents their theory better, and we deem the one theory true and the other not true, not on the merits of the theory but on the skill of the one who presents the theory. This is often the case in debates or courts of law.

Coherence theories are also relative to history. Many theories appear coherent until history reveals new data for which those theories are unable to give an account. This seems to be a very real part of our human condition. We create ways of making sense of our experience and treat those explanations as true until anomalies appear, and then we set out to find new theories or paradigms that can create a more coherent picture that better accounts for the new data. This is what is behind the history of civilization and what has caused the modern mind to evolve into something very different from the minds of our ancestors.

Pierce and James

In light of the difficulties facing both the correspondence and coherence theories, it is not surprising that a third theory emerged in the nineteenth century. Charles Sanders Peirce (1839-1914) and William James (1842-1910) were two Harvard professors who suggested that perhaps a better way to think about truth was whether a certain idea worked or not; that is, whether it gave us the results we desire. In other words, ideas or propositions that were fruitful were true and those that were not fruitful were not true. Thinking of truth in terms of fruit rather than facticity (correspondence) or clear and distinct ideas (coherence) at first seems strange since we have learned to think about truth as something impersonal and objective. Of course, as we saw in the last chapter, Kierkegaard had already started to rethink truth in terms of personal or subjective experience, and people like Pierce and James were moving in that same direction.

The philosophical perspectives of the past tried to convince us that we all saw the same world because of an active intellect (Aristotle), or because clear and distinct ideas like seven or circle are the same for all of us (Descartes), or we all have the same innate mental hardware through which to process our experience (Kant). We were happy to inherit these perspectives since they gave us a sense that we were not alone in our truth, but both existentialism and pragmatism cast doubt upon notions of universal truth in favor of a truth that was subjective and personal. We have always wanted our ideas of goodness, beauty, and truth to be like our concepts of seven or circle. Our concepts of seven and circle are clear and distinct but they are not the concepts that shape our lives like our ideas of goodness, beauty, and truth, which are mysterious concepts that seem to defy definition because they are so personal. Plato's hope was that philosophy could bring us to know such things in the same way we know mathematical or geometrical concepts but that has not happened and, by the nineteenth century, we started to move away from such an ambition and embrace such concepts on a more personal level. At the end of our lives what seems to define a person are not objective and universal concepts but rather what they personally held to be good, beautiful, and true. These personal concepts are what shape our lives, and the way to judge all three is by seeing what kind of fruit those concepts yielded. When we want to know a person, we want to know what they personally think is good and beautiful, if our ideas of goodness and beauty are personal, why not truth as well? Something like this is the basis for pragmatic thinking, and the basis for William James' concept of truth.

Like Kierkegaard, James thought that truth had to be personal and if it was not, it was something other than true. James says that the only question that should matter concerning truth is what difference does it make whether this particular idea is true or not? If it does not matter, why are we concerned with it? Truth should be a matter of personal concern and trivial matters should not receive consideration as being true. To reduce truth to facticity or clarity is to trivialize truth. James tells an interesting story to illustrate this point. He had been camping with some friends and upon returning from a hike, there was a discussion underway concerning a certain squirrel. Several campers had seen a squirrel place itself behind a tree so the campers could not see it. When the campers moved to one side of the tree to see the squirrel, the squirrel moved to keep the tree between itself and the campers. The campers continued to move around the tree and so did the squirrel. When the campers had circumnavigated the tree, the question arose whether they had gone around the squirrel. Some said yes, since they had circumnavigated the squirrel, but others said no, since they had not lapped the squirrel and the squirrel had always stayed ahead of them. We should take two things from this story: First, our understanding is relative to how we conceptualize something like the idea of "going around something." Second, what difference does it make if this or that particular understanding is true.

On the first point, James was becoming aware of how our notion of truth was dependent upon perspective, which in turn was dependent upon language and what it meant to "go around" something. We could argue about this and try to resolve the conflict by defining "go around" the way we define a circle or seven, but would that really be getting at the truth of the matter or would it just be settling on some convention? His second point is related but more salient: does it really matter whether you went around the squirrel or not? To consider such a matter as one that is pursuing truth is to trivialize truth. Truth has to be more impactful.

If truth should matter, then the first question is what difference would it make if it were true or not? If we answer, that it would make no difference, than it is not a question of truth. If truth is to be meaningful like goodness and beauty, it has to have the same kind of weightiness as goodness and beauty and cannot be concerned with trivial matters. Thus, James claims that the first and only question that philosophers should ask concerning truth is what consequences follow if this thing is true. Of course, this was a rather radical notion of truth. We had always wanted to connect truth to something greater than our own perspective and the consequences of our beliefs, but by the nineteenth century, such a transcendent truth seemed to be beyond our reach. In light of this, pragmatism seemed an attractive way to conceptualize truth.

Another interesting aspect of pragmatism was its connection to faith. Throughout the modern period, reason was supreme. Recall how eighteenth century critics of David Hume accused him of atheism, not because he did not believe in God but because he did not believe in a rational faith. Also recall our earlier mention of the fact that by the nineteenth century some had gone so far as to claim that it was immoral to hold beliefs that had no support in reason. James thought that a belief prior to evidence was often required in order to open the possibility for evidence. For James, the dominant scientific notion that we get at truth objectively by laying down our biases and refusing to believe anything before we have evidence for that belief is the strangest notion imaginable and life simply does not work that way. If a man wants to know if a particular woman loves him, he has to begin with the belief and faith that she will. Without that initial belief or faith, he will not act and the evidence will never come. Likewise, a politician has no evidence that he can win an election and, in fact, odds are against him, but his belief is contagious and people start to believe in his vision and the consequence is that he wins the election. Belief in many situations makes possible the emergence of truth. This is not to say that believing makes it so or that believing is the sole cause of truth, but without believing, the truth does not have a chance to emerge. Even hard science begins with beliefs they call hypotheses. Of course, the hardcore scientific community of James' day argued that they quickly abandon those beliefs or hypotheses if the evidence to support them is not forthcoming. The history of science, however, is full of examples of people staying with their hypotheses without supporting evidence long after it was reasonable and only in the end to have their belief validated by evidence.

We would like to believe that we have evidence for the things we believe and that it is not rational to believe things for which we do not have evidence. That would certainly make us feel secure in what we know, but what the history of our evolving human condition reveals is that at the base of all we know or purport to know are beliefs without evidence. Philosophers in the twentieth century will almost universally agree that we are entitled to our basic beliefs because without them knowledge has no basis. All of our knowledge is ultimately traceable to beliefs that we cannot verify or falsify with any evidence other than the consequences they yield. To eliminate beliefs that have no evidence apart from their consequences is to eliminate the basis for all knowledge.

Another interesting aspect of pragmatism is that it is able to get at certain questions that leave other theories of truth stymied. For example, there is the question of whether human beings possess a free will or whether our lives are determined. There are several ways to deal with this and there is evidence to support both sides. Medieval philosophy was obsessed with this and philosophers felt compelled to take sides in the debate. The medieval debate was set in theological terms. If God is sovereign and determines all things, it does not seem that human beings are free, and if not free, how can God judge us for things over which we have no control? On the other hand, if we are free and do determine our own fate, does that mean that God is not sovereign?

Getting at the truth of this matter from a correspondence or coherence theory of truth is fruitless, so James considers the question from a very different direction. Pragmatically, will we be better people if we believe in free will or determinism? James argues that free will produces more fruit and we will be better people if we believe in free will rather than determinism. Of course, some people assume too much responsibility for themselves and others, and perhaps they would do better to believe more in God's sovereignty than the idea that everything rested upon an individual's shoulders. On the other hand, some people trust God's sovereignty to such an extreme that they lack initiative and responsibility, so perhaps on this matter truth is more personal than even James imagines.

Like Kierkegaard, James introduced us to a concept of truth that is more subjective and personal, and like Kierkegaard, this pragmatic notion of truth could have its greatest application in the area of religion. At present, there are thousands of Christian denominations worldwide, each professing that they have the most coherent interpretation of the teachings of the One they claim to follow. They have constructed enormous theologies in order to make their interpretation of Christianity seem the most coherent. By contrast, pragmatism ignores the coherence of their theologies and looks to the consequences of their beliefs to see if those beliefs produces lives that replicated the life of the One they claim to follow. Jesus seems to endorse such a pragmatic concept of truth when he says, "You will know them by their fruits."[13] A good theology is one that bears good fruit, and bad theology bears bad fruit. A pragmatic theology is one judged by the consequence of how closely our lives reflect the life of whom we claim to follow. Jesus never gave us any kind of theology but rather a life for us to model. Thus, a particular theology is true to the extent that it makes us more like the Divine. An interesting consequence of such a theology is that if someone professes to believe a certain religious doctrine, but that doctrine has no affect or consequence upon their lives, it is not a true belief at all but merely an opinion about a squirrel going around a tree.

---

13. Matt. 7:16.

Like Kierkegaard, James thought that our connection to truth was deeply personal and subjective. Of course, many people find such a personal and subjective truth terrifying and want the security that comes from believing that what they believe is a universal truth. We want truth to be like mathematics and when someone suggests it is not, we often respond violently. In medieval Europe, we burned the avant-garde and heretic alive in order to suppress anything that threatened the illusion of a universal truth and the security that came from that belief. In the twentieth century, we saw the rise of fascist regimes and ethnic cleansing as attempts to silence the voices of those who threaten our illusions.

CHAPTER NINE

Authenticity and Hermeneutics: Martin Heidegger and Hans-Georg Gadamer

One of the criteria by which we judge the greatness of philosophers is how successful they were at attacking and offering alternatives to some of our most elemental ideas and basic concepts. By that criterion, Martin Heidegger (1889–1976) is considered by many to have been the most original philosopher of the twentieth century.

Since the time of Plato and Aristotle, philosophy has focused on epistemology or the question of knowledge. In their quest for knowledge, Plato, Aristotle, and nearly everyone else, imagined that we are sensate, rational subjects trying to know the world of objects that surround us. Heidegger realized that paradigm was no longer adequate since we had become increasingly aware of the fact that much of what we experience does not come from the objects of our experience but from what we bring to those objects. What he suggested was that instead of pursuing knowledge we return to the earlier Pre-Socratic preoccupation with ontology or being itself; that is, rather than trying to know an objective world, Heidegger wanted to know what it meant for human beings to *be* in the world. Heidegger describes this *being* in the world as engagement, which is very different from the kind of knowing that philosophy has traditionally practiced.

In order to explain this concept of engagement, Heidegger used the German word, *dasein* (literally, being there). Dasein represents the unique way that human beings are in the world, and that *being in the world* is very different from the way we learned to think about the world. Heidegger claimed that the subject/object distinction that had been the cornerstone of Western thought presented us with an unrealistic picture of thinking subjects encountering a world of objects. That is not how we experience the world but rather how we like to think about our experience, since it gave us the idea that we could know things objectively or as they are in themselves. That, however, never happens and we always encounter things as our minds construct them.

Since the time of Kant, we have known that we bring something to our experience, and with the history that followed Kant, we have come to realize that what we bring to that experience is much more than the innate mental hardware that Kant imagined. We also bring a host of concepts that had their origin in the philosophical imaginations of our ancestors; we acquired them, however, not as philosophical concepts but as an inheritance from our history, culture, and language communities. Thus, our engagement with the world is not that of a subject encountering objects but as one interpreting data through a host of historical, cultural, and linguistic concepts that constitute the prejudices through which we interpret everything. Before we understood that these prejudices were far more extensive than we imagined, early modern science maintained that we could simply eliminate our prejudices and thereby get at things in their objective state. Although the legacy of early modern thinkers would persist for centuries, Kant, and what followed in Kant's wake, revealed that we could never eliminate all that we brought to our experience. Perhaps a newborn experiences pure data, or at least data encumbered only by the kind of native hardware of which Kant spoke, but acculturation and language acquisition quickly begin to impose a meaning upon such data. Much of the understanding we acquire through acculturation and language acquisition is philosophical in nature in that it originated in someone's imagination in order to make sense of their experience. We now know that we can never get rid of the philosophical prejudices through which we interpret our experience. The best we can do is to replace our prejudices with better ones. This is the philosophical nature of our species, which Heidegger and his student Hans-Georg Gadamer realized and attempted to illumine.

In rejecting our prejudice toward the subject/object distinction, Heidegger took us in a very different direction and attempted to explain the world as we actually encounter it. For Heidegger, the aim was not to understand things independent of our awareness of them but as we experience them or as they are for us. It is not exploring reality objectively but rather as human beings experience it. Many may still be under the legacy of early modern science and attempt to know an objective world independent of the human self that perceives it, but Heidegger began with the much more realistic concept of engagement. Engagement is not about how we know the world but about how we experience it, or should experience it. This represented an enormous change in philosophy from the epistemological perspective that has been in effect since the time of Plato and Aristotle, to the early ontological tradition of the Pre-Socratic philosophers. Ontology is the study of being rather than of knowledge, but Heidegger claimed that there are really two very different notions of being, which he designated as little b being and big B being. The little b beings are the objects of the world which had previously been the objects of our thought. But Heidegger wanted to focus on big B being or existence as human beings experience it. Being human is not like being a chair, a tree, or even a mammal. We exist in time like no other creatures and this is what creates our human angst. Our existence has a horizon, which is our awareness of our own impending death. This awareness makes our knowing of our own existence or Being unlike knowing anything else. We can know a math problem or know an historical fact, or even another person, but to know that our existence has a horizon and to know ourselves in light of that reality is like no other kind of knowing. Most people avoid knowing themselves in that light at all cost. If they do spend any extended time contemplating their own horizon (death), they usually resort to some religious formula for eternal life and convince themselves that their horizon is not really a horizon at all.

Heidegger thought that because most people seek to avoid this reality of their own Being, they live in a state of what he calls *verfallen*. *Verfallen* is the radical deprivation of the human condition. This fallen-ness from knowledge of our actual Being is due at least in part to language, which Heidegger claims is the "house of being." Our language and therefore thinking has focused our attention on little b being instead of what it means to be human. The given state that we inherit from our language community and history is a fallen state focused on all the little distractions that keep us from engagement with life itself. In order to overcome this fallen state, we must focus our attention on the most classic and ancient question of philosophy; that is, the meaning of life. He thought this is the ultimate business of philosophy and the ultimate business of being human, but his ambition is not to find the universal meaning of life, but to find an authentic meaning that is true for himself. Engagement with life is meant to produce an authentic truth similar to the personal truth of which Kierkegaard spoke—a truth for which we might live and die. Authenticity is Heidegger's answer to the existential dilemma in a similar way that subjective truth was for Kierkegaard and rebellion was for Camus. What Heidegger is proposing is that our choice in life is either to accept the meaning and purpose that our culture and history provide, or to set out on an authentic journey to find what is true for us as individuals. If we accept the music, art, philosophies, and theologies of the tradition we inherit, we find great security in believing that those traditions are true because they are believed by great numbers of people, but such security comes at a high price. It means we are less than authentic and are refusing to address the most important question: what is the meaning of *my* life? When individuals take that question seriously, they set out on an intellectual and spiritual journey in order to find the music, art, philosophies, and theologies that are true for them—that resonate with their big B Being. This is also what is at the base of the philosophical imagination. We become philosophical when our inherited understanding can no longer account for our experience and we are forced to create for ourselves an authentic understanding capable of giving meaning to our experience. In a sense, Heidegger thought that what it means to be human is to become philosophical and refuse to retreat into the security of the herd. Our *verfallen* state mistakenly causes us to believe in a universal, objective truth that we can know and feel secure about. We support that delusion by finding great numbers of people who believe the same things we do, but that is all part of our fallen-ness.

Heidegger's philosophy is certainly an ethic, but not in the traditional sense. It does not deal with morality as we generally understand it, but it is an ethic in that it speaks of how we *ought to be* in the world rather than how we are in the world. All of science and much of philosophy deal with the way things are, or the way we think things are, but ethics deals with what ought to be rather than what is. In that regard, Heidegger certainly presented an ethical principle concerning how we ought to be in the world. It is, however, an existential ethic in that it does not offer some universal standard of behavior. Rather, it summons us to face the ultimate reality of our Being and to live authentically, refusing to slip back into the herd, focusing our attention on all the little distractions that keep us from facing the ultimate reality of our existence. That ultimate reality is that our lives do not go on forever but have a horizon in our individual deaths, at which time we must answer the philosophical question concerning the meaning of life. It is, however, an existential question of what your individual, particular life meant to you. What was the truth you learned to live for?

Authenticity is Heidegger's answer to the existential question of meaning. Most people find meaning in the prejudices they inherit; that is, that wealth, pleasure, career, or family will provide an individual with a meaningful existence. Indeed, it often does, or at least it does until one contemplates their own nonexistence.

The contemplation of one's own death reveals the emptiness of wealth, pleasure, careers, and even family. For Heidegger, meaning could only come out of one's authentic engagement with life and refusal to accept what was offered as meaning to the herd. Thus, Heidegger's ethic is quite different from traditional notions of ethics. It is about a personal encounter with life, God, and other human beings. Such an encounter, as Kierkegaard says, produces fear and trembling. That fear makes us want to retreat into the security of finding others who believe what we believe, rather than to create an authentic existence.

Not surprisingly, Heidegger's work and especially his ideas of engagement and authenticity have had their greatest impact upon existentialists in the twentieth century. What might be more surprising is the fact that the other area of great impact has been that of theology. In the twentieth century, theologians like Paul Tillich, Rudolph Bultmann, and Karl Rahner began to talk about God not as an object to be known but as engagement. We may study the attributes of a particular object like a table or chair in order to know it, but we are not engaged with it. Our scientific model for knowing supposes that the ideal way to know something is as an object independent of any subjective influences that we may bring to our examination of that object. That, however, is not the way we know a person. Knowing a person comes about through engagement: feeling what they feel and knowing as they know. Several twentieth century theologians suggested that this is a more appropriate way to encounter and know God.

Heidegger was certainly opposed to theology especially as it has existed in the modern era, but he was not opposed to the idea of God. What he did object to was the God of the philosophers and theologians. The God of the philosophers and theologians is an epistemological God who is the object of our knowledge. The God of the Bible, on the other hand, is an experiential rather than theological God. It is story after story of human beings' authentic engagement with God. It is about people having authentic encounters with God, and out of that authentic experience, creating a personal understanding of God and themselves. Theologies are created later by people who merely think about those experiences second hand and try to make universal truths out of them.

Part of our *verfallen* human tendency is to objectify and universalize both our experience and the meaning we attribute to that experience in order to make it appear substantial and more than our own individual experience. This is especially true of spiritual experiences. In theistic religions, which personify God and speak of a personal relationship with that God, it is impossible to establish a universal understanding, just as it is impossible to create a universal understanding of any person. Personal knowledge is always unique and authentic. No two people know you, or any other person, the same way. If we personify God, the same is true of God. Amazingly, people who have authentic religious experiences often turn around and deny others a similar authentic experience because it does not replicate their own experience. We create objective theologies and insist that other's encounters with the Divine must take place within the same parameters established by our theology. There was a time when it might have been natural to think that we should measure our lives by a universal standard that we either meet or fail to meet, but Heidegger points toward an authentic truth that represents a higher level of consciousness.

Gadamer

Heidegger had many famous students, but Hans-Georg Gadamer has to be in the top tier. Like Heidegger, he was opposed to positivist science that limited the scope of science to a rigid method based upon the subject/object distinction. Like his teacher, he also tried to advance the idea that life should be lived as engagement rather than as perceiving subjects experiencing an objective world. Gadamer's great contribution in this area was to attempt to develop some insight into how best to proceed in understanding the world as engagement.

Gadamer criticized positivist science because it reduced truth to something that could be accessed only by math or hard science. The parables of Jesus and the works of Shakespeare are true although neither is true by Descartes' criterion of clear and distinct ideas or sciences' idea of facticity. Both Descartes and modern science gave us methods to arrive at truth, but Gadamer claimed that if we are thinking of truth as something that only math and science can deal with, we are living very shallow lives largely devoid of truth. When we wish to know anything, we are after truth, but not necessarily truth in the limited sense of certainty or facticity. We are in pursuit of truth when we wish to know: a piece of literature, another person, the game of baseball, or how to mother or father a child. When a psychoanalyst attempts to know a person's psychological state they are pursuing truth, just as when we seek to know the true interpretation of a poem. Of course, in many of these cases there could be more than a single truth. There may be multiple diagnoses for a patient, and there may be more than a single interpretation of a poem. In the case of the poem, the fact that there is more than a single true interpretation might stand as part of its greatness. To insist that there can only be one truth in such cases is extremely narrow-minded and truncates our view of truth and reality. Of course, such a narrow notion of truth is quite common, although largely due to the cultural influences of mathematics and the hard sciences upon our education. Such an education, and the notion of truth it fosters is meant to prepare us to be productive members of the economy, but Gadamer thinks that education and truth should have a humanizing effect upon us.

To get at such a humanizing truth requires a method, but a method very different from that of the sciences. In fact, it is the very opposite of the classic scientific method in that while science attempted to eliminate all prejudices within the perceiving subject in order to get at an objective truth, Gadamer's method uses the prejudices of the individual to get at the truth. Indeed, our prejudices are precisely what allow us to become immersed in the truth of what we want to know. Without the prejudices we inherit from our culture and history we have no way of beginning an inquiry into anything. Newborns perceive the world but there is no meaning or understanding to what they perceive. Only our inherited prejudices that we acquire through socialization, language acquisition, and early learning give us the philosophical perspectives and concepts we need to form some type of understanding. Thus, our prejudices are essential to any pursuit of truth. Gadamer, however, makes a distinction between enabling prejudices and bad prejudices. Our prejudices are good if they are open rather than closed; that is, they are good in that they give us access to the world, but bad if we imagine them to represent truth itself which makes them into prejudices that prevent us from going into deeper interpretations of our experience. Thus, prejudices are good because they give us access to the world but they become bad if we do not allow our prejudices to change in order to get at deeper and richer interpretations of our experience.

Many people get a great sense of security by believing that their prejudices are truth itself rather than a first step toward truth. Our prejudices are what enable us to immerse ourselves in something; immersion or engagement is required and is very different from the cool indifference and pretense to objectivity of modern science. We come to know the game of basketball not through objective study and analysis, but by getting immersed in it. A game or a piece of music requires spirit in order to get at its truth. Of course, spirit is exactly what modern science wanted to eliminate. Science prizes unbiased observation in order not to prejudice the outcome. Life, however, is not something we impartially observe but something in which we participate. A great piece of music is not something we observe, but something in which we become immersed. We can know the truth of that music on many levels. Some may know all the words to a song, but someone else gets lost in it and knows the song on a deeper level. This deeper level of knowing the truth through engagement with life requires immersion. The way Gadamer suggests we pursue this deeper truth is through a hermeneutic dialogue.

The term hermeneutics originally referred to the study of the way we interpret texts. It began with the study of biblical and legal texts and, up until the twentieth century, most who studied hermeneutics were intent upon finding a method in order to get at an ultimate and univocal meaning of a text. Hermeneutic methods based upon the subject/object distinction center on eliminating the subjective element in order to get at an objective understanding.

By the twentieth century, however, it had become obvious that the subjective element, or what we bring to our experience, was much too vast to simply eliminate. Furthermore, Gadamer suggests we begin with our prejudices since they are precisely what give us access to the world and make some sense of our engagement with it. What we are trying to do is not to eliminate our prejudices but to be open to changing them in order to get a better reading of the experience.

Gadamer's hermeneutics is not like traditional biblical hermeneutics in that the latter had traditionally used a variation of a modern scientific method that tried to eliminate the subjective biases of the scholar in order to get at the ultimate or objective meaning of the text. Of course, this presupposes both the subject/object distinction and the assumption that there is one single ultimate meaning to the text. What Gadamer suggested is something very different. He acknowledged our prejudices since they are what give us access to what we are trying to understand, but instead of insisting that what we are experiencing conforms to our prejudices, we should trust our authentic experience to transform our prejudices. If we trust our authentic experience rather than the prejudices of our conventional understanding, those experiences have the power to change our prejudices. Thus, with a new understanding in place, because of our reformed prejudices, we are open to new experiences that were previous hidden by our earlier prejudices. As we continue to allow new experiences to change the prejudices of our conceptual understanding, we are continually renewing our minds and with those new prejudices, we are able to make sense of data previously unseen or ignored. In a very real way, our minds tell us what to see. It is not that our minds create the world but rather that they transform it. What Gadamer suggested is that the hermeneutic circle reforms what is before us in order to make sense of data that our inherited minds and their prejudices could not. The hope is that this hermeneutic circle, or perhaps it is better phrased "hermeneutic spiral," will lead us deeper and deeper into authentic truth. This is very different from a hermeneutic that seeks a univocal meaning. Great texts generally contain meaning on multiple levels. Plato and Aristotle understood this but it was for the most part lost on the modern world, which exalted the mathematical model and insisted upon a single answer to every question.

Of course, what Gadamer suggested with the hermeneutic circle is very different from our normal thinking, but it is what lies at the very base of philosophical intelligence. Under normal circumstances we use the prejudices that make up our understanding to judge whether something is true. If data conform to our prejudices, we deem them true and if they are incompatible with our prejudices, we reject the data as not true. On occasion, however, we are confronted with data that are hard to reject in spite of the fact that they do not conform to our prejudicial understanding. In those cases, we can either ignore the data in order to preserve our prejudices and the false security that comes from imagining that those prejudices are truth itself rather than the product of someone else's philosophical imagination, or seek to change our prejudices in order to accommodate the data we deem of more worth than our prejudices. As we have seen throughout this text, philosophical thinking is essentially a matter of coming up with new prejudices that will better account for certain compelling data. What has always restricted the philosophical imagination is the belief that a certain conceptual prejudice is not a prejudice at all, but truth itself. As we have said, such a belief provides a sense of security, but such security comes at a high price. It stifles the imagination and gives us the erroneous idea that the world is as we perceive it. By contrast, human history moves forward because of the philosophical imagination at work within the hermeneutic circle. History evolves because new prejudices or philosophical perspectives replace old one because they can give an account of certain data in a way that the old prejudices cannot. What we often refer to as scientific advances are most often actually new philosophical perspectives that open us to new ways of seeing the world.

Gadamer's notion of truth is much deeper than truth as either facticity or certainty. It is about getting at the meaning of a thing. Meaning is not some eternal and immutable form but something that emerges over time for us, both as individuals and as a species. It is unique to individuals and their time and place. Aristotle has a different meaning to me than he had for Thomas Aquinas. This does not mean that truth is relative, but it does mean that different perspectives allow for different insights and the possibility of different meanings. The meaning I attribute to *Oedipus the King* is different from the meaning its author attributed to it because I have the advantage of viewing it through Freud's perspective, which Sophocles lacked.

With the modern scientific model, we tried to understand things objectively. But what would it mean for historians to understand fifth century England objectively? Does it mean they would rid themselves of all the prejudices of a twenty-first century understanding and take on all the prejudices of fifth century England? Clearly, that is impossible. Additionally, why would we want an objective understanding of fifth century England? What would that mean? The ideal is not an objective view but an authentic view. An authentic view is one created out of the unique circumstances of one's life. It begins with the prejudices of one's inherited understanding, but proceeds by altering, adjusting, and replacing those inherited prejudices with ones that provide more meaning for the uniqueness of our existence. The ultimate truth of our human condition is the truth we create for ourselves out of the circumstances of our lives.

The artist, musician, surgeon, mother, or priest are all trained, either formally or informally, according to some general prejudices that guide their activity in those areas. Initially, we need to consider these prejudices true in order to function in those areas. Some continue to cling to those truths all of their lives, but others see them for what they are. Consequently, on those occasions when a particular prejudice fails to account for a given situation, the philosophical imagination allows philosophically thinking individuals to form new ways of conceptualizing the experience.

As we have said, many people choose to cling to their inherited prejudices at all costs for fear of losing what they imagine to be truth. Others, however, allow the circumstances of their lives to change their inherited prejudices to account for a more personal truth which better reflects their own actual experience. If someone is not very interested in art, music, medicine, mothering, or God, their inherited prejudices concerning such usually serve them well. If, however, such things as art, music, medicine, children, or God are of great concern, their inherited prejudicial understanding eventually proves insufficient and they seek to change those prejudices into something that better reflect their unique experience. This is the authentic notion of truth of which Heidegger and Gadamer speak. It is a frightening truth since it requires that one leave the herd and the sense of security that so many find in believing that their way of conceptualizing their experience represents some objective and universal truth. Consequently, most choose either to cling to their inherited understanding or to quickly establish alternative prejudices and then cling to them as if they represented truth itself. The third option is to hold prejudices loosely in order that new data might alter them or even create entirely new ones. Such openness, however, requires a very different concept of truth. It is not a truth we can possess but a truth we can only pursue.

Of course, our inherited concept of truth as facticity or certainty gives us the illusion that truth is something we can possess. People feel secure in owning something and that is especially the case when it comes to truth, but that is a petty notion of truth, which produces arrogance, smugness, and the illusion of security. Although we would be much more comfortable with a truth that we can possess, such a truth is incompatible with what we now believe to be the nature of our human condition. We may not like the idea that we can never possess but only pursue truth, but it is also the most realistic stance given the enormous scope of the philosophical imagination, and the history of our previous prejudices' failure to endure.

CHAPTER TEN

The Linguistic Turn: Saussure, Wittgenstein, and Third Wave Feminism

Philosophers often refer to the twentieth century as the linguistic turn in philosophy. Language had always been important to philosophy. Aristotle trusted that language mirrored reality and revealed the basic structure of the world. That trust was progressively lost in the modern period. When moderns first peered into a microscope, what they saw at that level of experience was without a nomenclature, so they had to invent one. Of course, it was not simply a matter of naming things. What they were naming were kinds of things and thus they had to make decisions about what things were of the same kind. The fact that they had to invent a language on the microscopic level gave rise to the idea that language on the level of everyday experience might have come about in the same way. Add to this the fact that our modern exploration of remote parts of the world revealed that many native languages not only had different words but those words referred to different concepts than those of European languages. All this began to erode our trust that language somehow mirrored nature, and caused us to look at language in a new light. If

If language did not mirror nature, perhaps what we had considered metaphysical problems in the past were really problems about the nature and structure of language. This intensified our interest in language but that interest took us in two very different directions in the twentieth century. The one direction supposed that, since language shapes our minds to conceptualize the world in a certain way, we should shape language to improve the nature of our minds.

The German mathematician, logician, and philosopher, Friedrich Ludwig Gottlob Frege (1848–1925) developed a formal system of logic that could determine the validity of arguments with the same certainty as mathematics, and the British philosopher, Bertrand Russell (1872–1970) maintained that it is the philosopher's job to discover or invent a logically ideal language. From the Pre-Socratic philosophers Pythagoras and Parmenides and through Plato down to Descartes and the corpuscularians there have always been those who saw mathematics as the ideal for knowledge. At the beginning of the twentieth century, that tradition was kept alive by Frege and Russell.

At roughly the same time, however, the Swiss linguist Ferdinand de Saussure (1857–1913), regarded by many as the father of modern linguistics, began to explore language from a very different perspective. Instead of wanting to create a logically perfect language, he wanted to understand how language actually functioned in the real world. What he discovered was that words are much more arbitrary than we had imagined. Although we knew that language was more arbitrary than our ancient and medieval ancestors had imagined, we did not know how arbitrary until Saussure. What Saussure introduced was the idea that language is a world unto itself with much less correspondence to nature than we had realized.

Today, many people continue to believe that language is merely a matter of attaching words to kinds of things that have an actual existence in the world. Saussure provides a very different framework for understanding language that greatly undermines that view. He began with three concepts: the sign, the signifier, and the signified. The sign is the word, but words have two sides, much like a coin. The one side is the signifier, which is the sound bite, while the other side is the signified, or the concept to which the signifier refers. The bound between the two is arbitrary. There is no reason for the sound bite "dog" to be connected to the concept *dog* rather than *cat* other than that it is. Of course, that is not the case with onomatopoeia where the signifier and signified do seem to be intrinsically connected. In Plato's *Cratylus*, there is even speculation that all words were originally onomatopoetic, but that is wild speculation. Saussure claimed that onomatopoeias were "a fortuitous result of phonetic evolution."[14] It should also be obvious that the signifier or sound bite is arbitrary simply by considering languages where the same or very similar concepts have a great variety of different signifiers or soundbites.

Regarding the signified, although not arbitrary, they are not what we often imagine. Plato imagined that things were the kind they were because they shared a common essence or characteristic that reflected an otherworldly form. Aristotle placed these forms within things themselves and claimed that we possessed an active intellect capable of detecting these forms in order to group

---

14. Ferdinand de Saussure. *The Course in General Linguistics*. Trans. Wade Baskin (New York: Philosophical Library, 1959). 68.

things into the kinds to which we attach words. The corpuscular philosophy undermined that view, but there was still the lingering notion that words were somehow about real entities rather than merely ideas about how we might organize our understanding. We want to believe that mammals and human races actually exist and are not merely modern ways of organizing how we think and talk about the world, but Saussure was destroying that belief.

We had always imagined that the concepts that words or sound bites signified were atomic concepts with particular essences, but Saussure claimed that the signified only had meaning in reference to the rest of language, and there were no atomic essences at the base of language. He claimed that we do not learn language the way philosophers had always thought about language. Saussure claimed that we learn language structurally and, instead of knowing *cat* as an atomic concept based upon some essence, we instead know that cat is not dog or rat. Philosophers and dictionaries have led us in a wrong direction and the way we really learn language is not by learning the meaning of individual concepts. Rather we learn the meaning of a concept in reference to the rest of language. Recall Hegel and the idea that what something is not is what gives boundaries and dimensions to that thing. We define things more by their otherness than by some abstract definition. Of course, the same thing is true of the signifier or the other half of the word. We do not learn language by learning a particular sound bite in isolation from the rest of language, but in reference to other sound bites. The sound bite *cat* is different from rat or mat, and that is how we come to know how to use language.

Structuralism had an enormous affect upon many philosophers in the twentieth century, but one of the most interesting was

Ludwig Wittgenstein (1889–1951). Wittgenstein is interesting because he represents both traditions in twentieth century philosophy of language. Early in his career, he followed Russell and Frege in the pursuit of a logically perfect language. With the publication of his *Tractatus Logico-Philosophicus* in 1921, Wittgenstein established himself as one of the leading voices in that linguistic tradition. Strangely, however, after coming to great recognition and reputation in that tradition of linguistic philosophy, Wittgenstein changed directions. In *Philosophical Investigations* he set out to understand language not in some logically ideal form but as it actually exists among human beings.

Like Saussure, Wittgenstein realized that words do not have atomic meanings, and the Socratic quest for the immutable and eternal forms was misguided. Thus, just as Heidegger attacked the subject/object distinction, Wittgenstein challenged a very big idea; that although Western thinking since the time of Plato had equated words with forms or common characteristics that ran through an entire species, words do not require a common denominator, as Plato, and almost everyone since, has imagined. In Plato's *Meno*, Socrates asks Meno to think about the fact that words like courage, justice, temperance, and wisdom are all called virtue. How can we call them all by the same name unless there is some common characteristic or definition that they all share? Meno thinks about it and answers that Socrates must be right and there must be some common characteristic if we call them all by the same name. Wittgenstein turns things around and does not ask us to think, but to look; to look at what we call virtues and see if they have a common characteristic. We think they must, for what other explanation could there be? Well, Wittgenstein looked and did not see a common characteristic; so his philosophical imagination had to come up with something that will explain how language works if words do not have a common essence. What he developed is the idea of family resemblance.

In order to understand his idea of family resemblance, we have to begin with his understanding of language in general. In breaking from the way philosophers had always thought about language and focusing on the way people actually acquire language, Wittgenstein argued that we learn language the same way we learn to play games: that is, simply by doing it, making mistakes, and correcting those mistakes. Thus, although our thinking about language from Plato to the twentieth century was highly cerebral, the way that we originally acquire language is nothing like that. As children, we acquire language not by memorizing vocabulary and rules of grammar, but rather we simply mimick other members of the language community. If the members of the language community that we aped had good vocabularies and grammar, we acquired "good vocabularies" and "good grammar". Perhaps later educators might try to expand our vocabulary and our understanding of grammar through memorization, but that is not how we acquire language initially. Initially, we learn language the way we learn games, that is, by playing them. No one teaches us to play the game of baseball by sitting us down and reading the rules of baseball to us. We simply learn the game by playing it. If we have never played the game of Monopoly, and someone wants to teach us the game by reading the rules to us, our eyes glaze over and after a paragraph or two and we usually interject, "Let's just play." Likewise, it is common knowledge that the best way to learn a foreign language is to be immersed in a culture where everyone speaks that language.

If we learn language the same way we learn to play games, then the philosophical search for the essence or common characteristic that we thought was so essential to language since the time of Plato no longer has a prominent place. We do not need to know the exact definition of something in order to know what the word means. When asked to define a word, the average person gives examples, but is unable to come up with a definition. Socrates made his interlocutors feel that without a precise definition, they really did not know what a particular word meant, but that does not seem to be the case. If a person can use a word in several different contexts and others know what he is talking about, why would we believe that there is anything more to that word than its effective use? Such a belief is a vestige of Platonism and not essential to language.

Wittgenstein's point is that language does not require more than examples. The idea of knowing a dictionary definition or a Platonic essence does not mean that one knows the language better than the one who can use the language without knowing an exact meaning. To believe that the person who knows an exact definition of a word knows something more than the one who uses the language effectively, without knowing that exact definition, is to suppose that that word has some ultimate reality beyond an agreed upon means for us to express our feelings and thoughts.

We have a long tradition of imagining that words have ultimate meanings, as when someone says to another, "that is not what that word means." Who determines what that word means? It is a rule in a language game, but it is a game where the rules are ever changing in spite of our wanting them to be like mathematical words that seldom change. The pronouns *they* and *them* have long been considered plural pronouns but as we seek to express ourselves without designating a specific gender, those words have become more like the pronoun *you* which is both singular and plural. Language is a tool that we use to express our thought and feelings, but it is a very strange tool in that language, although greatly affected by changes in human thinking, also has a life of its own. No individual can decide to change language. We can invent new words, but which ones are eventually adopted into our language is something beyond our control since language itself decides. Equally, the changes in language seem to defy any kind of evolutionary pattern that we could use to predict future changes in language.

This is hard for people to understand. One of the reasons for that is that mathematics was, in a way, our first language. We learned counting very early and got the idea that numbers had very specific forms. They did not vary from culture to culture or from historical epoch to historical epoch. Likewise, philosophers from Plato to Russell thought this was ideal and should be the model for all language, but the great insights of Saussure and Wittgenstein were that language is nothing like mathematics. Language may be God-given, but the content of language is a human creation that takes on a life of its own. Aristotle wrongly believed that language gave us a map of the world and mirrored reality. We now know that is not true, but there is a connection between language and human consciousness. Often changes in human consciousness and the way we see the world affect language, and likewise, changes in language can affect human consciousness. Consequently, one of the most interesting aspects of the linguistic turn in philosophy has been to see how language affects our thinking and molds our consciousness, often on a level below our conscious awareness. In order to see how this happens we turn to another interesting development in twentieth century philosophy: feminism.

Feminism, at least as it has existed in the United States, has centered on three great movements. The first began in the middle of the nineteenth century and focused on equality with the primary goal of women obtaining the right to vote. The second movement again focused upon equality, and in the 1970s attempted to amend the Constitution of the United States. The Constitution condemned discrimination on the bases of race, religion, creed, and national origin, but did not condemn discrimination over sex or gender. The Equal Rights Amendment attempted to add sex and gender to the list. The amendment received a two-thirds majority in both houses of Congress but failed to get the needed approval of three-quarters of the states in order to become law. The movement was moderately successful, however, in that many states did change their constitutions to condemn discrimination over sex and gender.

Both suffrage and the Equal Rights Amendment were primarily political movements. The present state of feminism, however, is more philosophical than political. Often referred to as Third Wave Feminism, today's feminism sees sexism as something deeply rooted and requiring more than simply changing laws. Like racism, sexism is largely acquired on an unconscious level. It is no longer acceptable to parade racist or sexist attitudes, but racism and sexism continue to be part of our cultural consciousness largely because of language. As mentioned, human consciousness affects language, and in turn, language affects human consciousness. Because of the social effects of racism and sexism, minorities and women have had less of an effect upon shaping language than white males. Thus, language largely reflects the experiences of white males rather than minorities and women. Of course, because we all share a single language we too easily think of it as reflecting a universal human experience, just as mathematics reflects a universal human experience. Add to this the fact that many people still believe that language mirrors reality and we can see why today's feminists see the deep roots of sexism embedded in language.

What feminists today recognize and want to explore is how uniquely different the female experience is from the male experience. Unfortunately, the language they have been given is a language meant to express the experience of male sexuality, male spirituality, male morality, and male psychological development and maturation. Consequently, today the feminist focus is on influencing language and creating a philosophical perspective capable of expressing the uniquely female experience. Just as new philosophical perspectives have generally appeared in reaction to a discovered problem, feminist philosophy appears as a response to our twentieth century awareness of the fact that language does not reflect reality but rather a perspective and a male perspective at that.

This is a problem unique to women. Other marginalized groups such as racial and ethnic minorities are not affected by language to the extent that women are. That is because marginalized groups other than women generally have a language that is able to express their unique experience. Under colonialism, the British forbad the Irish to use their native language in an attempt to take away their voice. Women are a marginalized group that has never had a native language, and they are in more need of it than perhaps any other marginalized group, because the female experience is so radically different from the male experience.

This is what makes sexism so different from racism. Racism is contrived. The idea of race was the invention of Western colonialism five hundred years ago in order to justify genocide in the non-white parts of the world. There was no notion of race prior to five hundred years ago. We had always recognized that people were ethnically different, but the idea that people were biologically or physiologically different was an idea that dates only to the early beginnings of the modern period. Furthermore, in spite of all the racists' efforts, there simply are no biological or physiological differences between the races. Any differences between what we consider races are the result of social and economic factors; this, however, is not the condition for women. Women are inherently different from men in a host of areas, but although the woman's experience concerning things like sex, spirituality, morality, and maturation are enormously different from the male experience, she is unable to express that experience because her only language is one that is inherently male. Do we really think that if women had more influence over the formation of language that the words we use for sex would be the same words we use to express male aggression? The words that we commonly use for sex are the same words that we use to express anger and the desire to hurt someone. Much of today's pornography is about male aggression and women enjoying that aggression. If women were the dominant influence upon our culture and language, would pornography look like it does, or would words for sex be words that equally express aggression? The female sexual experience is completely different from the male experience; yet we have a language that purports to represent and express universal human experience. In truth, it largely expresses male experience.

Do we really believe that the female spiritual experience is the same as that of the male? If God told Sarah rather than Abraham to sacrifice their son Isaac, would her response have been the same kind of obedience that Abraham demonstrated? The story argues Abraham's obedience to God was praiseworthy. Sarah might see the same thing as evil. In the Middle Ages, St. Anselm taught that God was a power to be obeyed, while Dame Julian of Norwich wrote about her love for Jesus. Men have been raised to think that suppressing personal feelings is noble and God pleasing; women might think that men are largely devoid of feelings. The fact that we often read the story about Abraham and Isaac as an example of a universal value of religious obedience rather than the male privileging of an abstract concept of obedience over the life of a mother's son is a great example of how language can be sexist and privilege the male perspective. Women have had different sensibilities than men toward both the Divine and morality. Imagine how different religion might look if women rather than men were the main force behind language formation.

The same is true of morality. We generally think of morality as universal. That is, that the idea of goodness is the same for women as it is for men. We imagine that what is right and moral is not different for men than women, or at least, that is what men have told us. Immanuel Kant claimed that morality was an imperative that applied to all human beings. Kant thought that all human beings pursue the good by doing what we would want everyone to do in that same situation. Such reasoning creates a principle by which all human beings can pursue what is good, but women often know what is good because of a feeling to care for someone rather than a principle. If Kant had ever been married, perhaps he would have been convinced to think differently. Kant, however, does give us a great picture of male morality. For the man, morality is largely a matter of following universal moral principles, but for the woman morality is more about caring for the one in need. Nel Noddings has written extensively on this point.[15] She claims that female morality requires more than a principle. It requires the one cared for. Men may operate out of universal moral principles but a woman's morality comes out of a response to the "one cared for." It is about experiencing someone in need and responding to that need, not out of principle but because of a felt connection to another human being. Some men may sense this as well, but it is rare because men are more often interested in simply doing the right thing according to their reasoning and principles.

Caring is different from following a principle. Caring is something that is felt, principles are pondered. Principles are cold and universal. Caring is warm and personal. Noddings beautifully expressed this notion of female morality and spirituality as relational in a story about Pearl S. Buck's father and mother. Noddings quotes Buck talking about how different her father and mother were in terms of their morality and spirituality. Her father was a missionary in China who was full of religious zeal. Everything he did for his congregation was in the interest of their eternal state and a theology he believed to be sacred. Her mother was very different. Her morality and spirituality were all about her children,

---

15. Noddings, Nel. *Caring: A Feminist Approach to Ethics and Moral Education*. University of California Press; Second Edition. 2013.

how she cared for and delighted in them. When her mother died, her father was concerned about his wife's eternal state since she did not seem to have the religious zeal he did. When her father was close to death, he wrote a short biography of his life. It focused almost exclusively upon his work as a missionary. He did in one place mention his wife and listed his children's names but forgot to mention a son who had died at the age of six, and who was his wife's favorite.

In addition to morality and spirituality, women are enormously different from men in terms of maturation. Carol Gilligan's *In a Different Voice*[16] is a classic study in how different psychological maturation is in a woman rather than in a man. Gilligan studied numerous accounts of maturation and found that in men maturation into adulthood centered on separation and independence. It was essentially about their relationship to the social world and to work. When she began to study maturation in women, she found something very different. For women, maturation involved the kind of attachment necessary to maintain the human community. The woman's identity is in the context of relationship, while the man's is in the context of separation and independent self-expression.

Other areas where the female experience is drastically different from the male experience are too numerous to mention here, yet that experience is silenced by the fact that the language they inherit has been much more influenced by men and meant to express the male rather than the female experience. Likewise, the philosophical perspectives they inherit have come almost

---

16. Gilligan, Carol. *In a Different Voice: Psychological Theory and Women's Development*. Harvard University Press. 1982.

exclusively out of the male imagination. Try to name a female philosopher who has had great significance in molding the nature of our minds the way we have seen male philosophers doing throughout this book. Heidegger's famous line that "language is the house of being" has special meaning to women, who realize they are living in a house that is not their own.

Of course, many women will take exception to this and claim that they are no different from men. I am sure they genuinely feel that way, but the fact that they see sexuality, spirituality, morality, and maturation the same as men is the result of acculturation, assimilation, and the influence of a common sexist language to which they conform. Without a feminist philosophy and a language that is capable of expressing their uniquely female experience, that is their only choice.

Thus, women have finally come to realize their need of a language and philosophical perspective capable of making sense of their very different experience. We have seen corpuscular philosophy create a new perspective to account for what was beyond Aristotle's imagination. Likewise, Kant created a perspective to overcome Hume's skepticism, and Kierkegaard created a perspective to give meaning to his personal experience. It is now time for women to exercise their philosophical imagination and produce a perspective capable of giving voice to the female experience.

CHAPTER ELEVEN

The End of the Metanarrative: Thomas Kuhn and Jean-Francois Lyotard

In 1962, Thomas Kuhn (1922-1996) published one of the most important books of the twentieth century. *The Structure of Scientific Revolutions* pointed out a delusion we had been under at least since the time of the Enlightenment. What Kuhn explained was that scientific progress is not what we had thought. Kuhn charts each particular science and shows that the paradigms or philosophical perspectives out of which those sciences operate last only as long as they prove fruitful in saving the appearance and explaining the data before us. Inevitably, however, new data arise from our expanding awareness that confound the prevailing paradigm. This forces us to seek a new perspective or paradigm capable of explaining the new data. Thus, science is not, as we all too easily imagine, a progressive building of knowledge toward an eventual complete understanding of the world. Instead, at the base of all the sciences are paradigms or philosophical perspectives that we need to replace when they no longer account for the data at hand. Kuhn concludes that the idea that eventually we will come upon a paradigm or perspective that will give us the ultimate way to perceive the world is erroneous in principle. What could possibly be the test for having arrived at such an ultimate paradigm? The history of science has shown, and we have seen the same thing with the history of philosophy, that even if a paradigm lasts for a thousand years, eventually we discover data that reveal how insufficient that perspective is.

We do not receive this news well. We want to maintain the illusion that our perspectives and theories represent the world itself, rather than merely a particular way of looking at the world. Every generation all too easily assumes that their perspective has finally unlocked the great mystery before us. Of course, later generations laugh at their ancestors for holding such a perspective, but then naively believe, as their ancestors had, that they now have come to the perspective that will save the appearance for all time. With every new perspective that is able to give an account of what is before us, we imagine that we have finally discovered how the world really works.

The same naiveté exists within religion. Taking the Christian religion as an example, over the course of its two thousand year history, there have been enormous changes concerning the perspectives through which Christians have interpreted the raw data of their religion. Christianity's original form changed drastically when the Roman Emperor Constantine adopted Christianity as Rome's official religion. Christianity went from being a suppressed religion to the Emperor's religion. Emperors certainly interpret Jesus' teachings differently than the oppressed. Another enormous change occurred a thousand years ago with the great schism between East and West, or Constantinople and Rome. Although there was a great deal behind this split and the theologies that came out of it, it left the world with two very different views of Christianity. While the Eastern Church focused on divinization or becoming more like the Divine, the Western Church would focus more on morality and the avoidance of sin. Five hundred years after that, the Protestant Reformation brought another profound change at least to the Western Church with its emphasis on faith.[17] Eventually, that idea of faith became a matter of right beliefs and doctrine. Today there are over forty thousand Christian denominations worldwide, many of which have doctrines and beliefs that they purport to represent absolute truth.

Of course, the changes in religion are somewhat different from the changes in science. They both might change in response to new data that confound their earlier perspectives, but with religion, the data is often spiritual in nature and therefore not so obviously observed. We do see the effect of this, however, in the Bible as human consciousness slowly evolved from our inability to imagine anything more than a tribal god to one whose dominion is the universe itself rather than a particular tribe. We filter spiritual data, as we filter all data, through a perspective or understanding that changes over time. As with any experience, our God experiences have as much to do with what we bring to the experience as what God brings. Indeed, often our understanding of our God experience says more about our perspective than about God.

Thus, as we have seen our perspectives change throughout the history of philosophy, the same is true of science and religion as well. An understanding of the history of philosophy, science, and religion brought Jean-Francois Lyotard (1924–1998) to

---

17. See, Phyllis Tickle's, *The Great Emergence: How Christianity Changed and Why*. Baker Books, 2012.

declare the end of the metanarrative. What he argued was that in the past, it was easier to believe that Aristotle, Catholicism, Newtonian Science, Luther, Adam Smith, Marx, or Einstein had finally explained how the world worked, or at least part of it, but it is hard to be so naïve today. Today, enough history has passed to convince those aware of that history that we have been under the illusion that we are capable of figuring it all out. What we now know is that we will never be in a place to make such a declaration. Even if we should eventually come to the perfect way to conceptualize our experience, how could we know when we had reached such a point? In the past, certain paradigms or philosophical perspectives lasted for thousands of years before we finally saw that they ultimately failed to explain and make sense of all that we experience.

As we go further into the microscopic world or out into the macrocosm of the universe, new data put ever-greater demand upon our imagination to create perspectives able to account for such data. Likewise, history continues to reveal new data about our human condition, which in time forces us to take on new perspectives concerning ourselves. This is the great insight of our age. That does not mean that there is no truth, although that is how some interpret it, since they equate their perspective with truth itself. Our perspectives are certainly essential, and without them we have no understanding at all, but when we equate them with truth itself, we fall into idolatry. Today, many people who are unaware of the history of philosophy and the evolving consciousness it has produced, continue to revere their theologies and theories as idols, which they imagine represent God or the world, rather than merely a perspective through which we try to make sense of our experience.

What we have seen throughout this text is how natural it is for the human imagination to create perspectives that make sense of our experience. Having created these perspectives, it is also somewhat natural to make those perspectives into idols. This occurs because, although our perspectives had their origin in someone's imagination, most individuals do not come by their perspectives through the imagination. Rather, most of us acquire our perspectives as an inheritance from our culture and history. Add to this the fact that we receive this inheritance as children, when it is essential to our social and psychological wellbeing that we believe that our inherited orientation to the world is true, and it is easy to see why we revere our perspectives as idols.

In the ancient, medieval, and early modern worlds, we could more easily maintain our perspectives as idols, but an understanding of history has helped to destroy these illusions. We now know that our scientific theories, theologies, and philosophies are merely perspectives that originate in imagination and through which we make sense of our experience. There is nothing wrong with that and in fact, it is essential in order that we provide the next generation with some type of orientation to the world. However, the maturation of human consciousness entails that we eventually accept our perspectives for what they are and cease to worship them. Phenomenalism, historicism, existentialism, pragmatism, hermeneutics, and feminism have all contributed to ending the unrealistic hope of creating a metanarrative that represents something more than merely a perspective. An understanding of our developing human consciousness and the perspectives it produces should bring us to the point where we no longer have to kill Socrates or Jesus in order to preserve our pitifully provincial perspectives that we mistake for truth.

There is, however, another interesting consequence of our evolving consciousness. It has produced a diversity the likes of which the world has never seen. Most people think of diversity in ethnic and racial terms but history has revealed a much deeper diversity that has to do with the vast variety of perspectives through which twenty-first century people view the world. Today, some people retain for a lifetime the belief that the inherited perspective they received in childhood reflects reality itself. They may not know who Aristotle was, but they believe that language mirrors reality and that words are about actual things that exist in the world, as he did. Others may have gone as far as Newton and early modern science, but no further. They imagine that the world is as science tells them it is. Still others have gone as far as Kant but not much further, while yet others have included some combination of historicism, existentialism, pragmatism, hermeneutics or feminism into their own authentic perspective. With such diversity of perspectives, how are we to reason together? Perhaps there was a time when there was a common metanarrative that made traditional rational discourse possible, but that no longer appears to be the case in our time. History has engulfed us in this enormous plurality, and consequently the idea of commensurability or beginning to reason from a common epistemological perspective has been lost.

This is the present challenge to the philosophical imagination. Amid such diversity of perspectives, how are we to pursue truth? Of course, it is important to respect the perspectives of others but, more importantly, we must see our own perspectives for what they are. Because they have their origin in human imagination, they do not give us access to eternal truths and, in time, additional data will reveal their inadequacy. Without an awareness of the nature and history of philosophy, however, we can imagine whatever we like. Such ignorance is blissful since it allows us to believe that truth or ultimate knowledge is something we can possess, but that is a dangerous illusion. Fortunately, we can dispel that delusion with an awareness of the fact that our philosophies, theories, and theologies have their origin in human imagination and in time prove inadequate. Such awareness should convince us that absolute truth is forever beyond us.

Of course, all this is in reference to a specific form of truth. It is truth as Aristotle taught us to think about, that is, as an epistemological concept. Aristotle claimed that human beings were involved in making, doing, and knowing: when we make, we want to make what is beautiful; when we do, we want to do what is good; and when we know, we want to know what is true. Thus, we think of truth as simply something to know, devoid of any thought of what is good or beautiful. This truncated, epistemic notion of truth has dominated Western thought, but what we have come to realize over the last several centuries is that we know such a truth through a conceptual perspective that has its origin in human imagination and that perspective changes with the vicissitudes of history. Because of this, absolute truth, in terms of something to know, is an unrealistic aim. This is what the history of philosophy, science, and religion should teach us; as long as truth is simply something to know and believe it will always be rooted in imagination as we struggle to make sense of our expanding experience. That, however, does not mean that we should not pursue absolute truth as a larger ontological concept. The larger ontological concept of truth is not as susceptible to our changing conceptual perspectives the way epistemic truth is because this larger truth concerning our being is not simply about what *is* but about what is *beautiful* and *good* as well. Over the last two hundred years, there has been a movement toward such a larger concept of truth, and it is to that larger concept of truth that we now turn our attention.

CHAPTER TWELVE

Philosophy and Theology in the Twenty-first Century: Toward a Broader Concept of Truth

This book has been an attempt to familiarize the reader with the kind of philosophical intelligence that is at the base of original philosophical thinking. In doing so, we have laid out something of a history of the way the philosophical imagination has caused human consciousness to evolve in order to make sense of new data as it has appeared over our history. In the last chapter, we discussed the fact that we are living at a time when people experience the world through a host of historical perspectives, and therefore we are experiencing an enormous diversity the likes of which the world has never seen. We see this most evidently in our contemporary political situation where people are in such enormous disagreement that they do not seem to be talking about the same world, and indeed, they are not. Those unaware of the changes in human consciousness over the last several hundred years see a very different world than those aware of such changes.

Today, the great challenge for the philosophical imagination is to come up with a solution to this most pressing problem. The problem seems to rest upon the fact that our idea of truth is relative to a particular perspective or way of conceptualizing our experience. At the end of the last chapter we suggested that this might only be the case, however, with a particular notion of truth as the object of knowledge. Perhaps there is another notion of truth that is not merely something to know and therefore not as dependent upon particular conceptual perspectives. Indeed, over the last two centuries, a concept of truth has been emerging that is not as dependent upon the philosophical imagination, nor is it merely the object of knowledge.

With Kierkegaard and the idea of existentialism, we began to see a notion of truth very different from what had dominated Western thinking since the time of Aristotle. Kierkegaard realized that the notion of truth that he had inherited was nothing like the truth that he actually experienced. For Kierkegaard, truth was something, as he says, "for which he might live or die." It was not a cold and naked truth that was simply something to know and believe, but a truth that he experienced as good and beautiful as well as true. It was a truth known through a direct experience rather than an intellectual perspective. In fact, from any purely intellectual perspective, it was absurd, but equally undeniable.

Likewise, with William James and the idea of pragmatic truth, our thoughts of truth are not simply about some ultimate reality that is the object of knowledge. When we reason pragmatically about truth, we take into consideration the outcome of what we deem true and such considerations involve our ideas of what is good or beautiful. When we think of truth as simply something to know regardless of its effect upon us, considerations of what is good or beautiful are absent. Recall James' point about the essential question of philosophy being, "What difference does it make if this or that particular matter is true?" If it makes no difference, it is a trivial matter and we should not speak of it in terms of truth. Of course, if it does make a difference, it necessarily involves notions of what is good or beautiful.

The rise of the social sciences in the nineteenth century also began to break from the idea of truth as simply something to know. Although earlier attempts at social science followed the model of the natural sciences and Aristotle's notion of truth as something simply to know, men like Karl Marx (1818–1883) and Max Weber (1864–1920) the founders of the discipline of sociology, realized that truth in the social sciences was unlike truth in the natural sciences. Marx's idea of a true social order was not simply factual but was what ought to be. Unlike the natural sciences, which seek simply to explain an actual state of affairs, Marx sought to point toward a more ideal truth that included his ideas of what was good and beautiful. We can debate whether his ideas were in fact good or beautiful, but the point is that his notion of truth was no longer simply something to know. In the same vein, Max Weber argued that we could not study the human realm without having ethical and aesthetic feelings aroused within us. Even if achievable, a social science that pursued a truth that was simply something to know would have a dehumanizing affect upon us.

The same is true of other social and behavioral sciences like anthropology and psychology. Since their subject matter is human beings, the question of what is good and beautiful is always directly present in a way that it is not present with hard sciences like geology, physics, chemistry, or astronomy. Of course, the hard sciences claim that such considerations would make their science less than objective, as if their science was not already less than objective because of the ever-changing perspectives that lie at the base of all human knowledge. Perhaps if the natural sciences had taken into account ethical and aesthetic considerations, the world wars of the twentieth century would not have been as brutal as they were and our environment would not be as threatened as it is. The perspectives through which we interpret and make sense of our experience will always be traceable to human imagination, and if we do not consider what is good and beautiful when creating those perspectives we are creating a barbaric inheritance for our children's children.

None of the sciences is objective in the sense of being independent of a perspective that came out of human imagination. The real difference between the natural and social sciences is that the natural sciences have simply addressed a truncated notion of truth as simply something to know, while the social sciences have addressed a larger ontological notion of truth because what they want to know concerns the very truth of our being.

In the twentieth century, Heidegger championed this notion of a larger, ontological truth, which was not simply something to know but something to Be. He replaced the epistemic notion of truth as subjects wanting to know objects with the idea of truth as a way to be in the world. Thinking about the world, and being in the world are two very different things, with two very different notions of truth. Heidegger pointed out that Being in the world involves a personal disposition or mood. Of course, enlightenment science insisted on eliminating such human elements in order to know reality objectively. We imagine that our particular mood should not affect the truth of what we know, but it does affect the truth of who we are. The truth of our being is much broader than the narrow truth of merely something to know, and it involves a host of elements that the hard sciences seek to eliminate in order to create the illusion of objectivity. We now know that such a perspective represents a narrow notion of truth, which can have a dehumanizing affect upon us.

In response to this truncated notion of truth we have inherited from the hard sciences, Hans-Georg Gadamer sought to extend our notion of truth to include the arts and humanities. He claimed that we needed to see things like the writings of Shakespeare or the parables of Jesus as true, not because they were factual but because they spoke of what is eternally good and beautiful. According to Gadamer, truth should have a humanizing effect upon us.

The linguistic turn of the twentieth century gave us even more reason to question the idea of truth as simply something to know. By the twentieth century, we were a long way from Aristotle and the idea that language mirrored nature. Saussure, Wittgenstein, and a host of others convinced us that language is our way of speaking about our experience and reflects what is in our heads rather than what is in the world. If language mirrored nature, as Aristotle had imagined, perhaps we could get to a truth that was simply something to know, but if language is about how we experience the world, truth must involve more than mere knowing, since our experience is not simply a matter of knowing.

Much of the thinking of the last two hundred years has been toward a larger notion of truth. Such a larger notion of truth, however, is hardly a new idea. In fact, such an ontological notion concerning the truth of our being was the notion of truth that occupied the thought of the Pre-Socratic philosophers that preceded Plato and Aristotle. They were concerned with the original question of philosophy concerning the meaning of life. The answer to that question is not something we simply know because it corresponds to facts or makes sense. Truth as something to know changes as the appearance of new data forces us to change our perspectives to accommodate that new data, but the larger truth that includes what is beautiful and good transcends our conceptual understanding and speaks to something deeper and more mysterious at the core of our being. Although our modern thinking until recently has ignored this question and focused almost exclusively upon mere knowing, this deeper notion of truth has been the focus of nearly all the great spiritual teachers throughout the ages. The great spiritual teachers in most traditions do not offer simply something to know and believe but a true way to be good and beautiful.

Originally, the Christian religion had such a truth at its core. It was not about knowing and believing certain doctrines or theologies, but about a certain way to *be*. In fact, originally, before we came to know it as Christianity, it was referred to as *The Way*. Jesus said, "I am the way, and the truth, and the life."[18] It was not a truth to know but a true way to be. It was about a way of life that was true because it was rooted in a goodness and beauty so divine that it allowed those who embraced its truth to treat others as they wished others to treat them.[19] It was a truth so divinely good and beautiful that those who embraced it loved even their enemies and gave to others without expecting anything in return.[20] It was a truth so divinely good and beautiful that those who fell in love

---

18. John 14:6.
19. Matt. 7:12. This also appears in all of the major world religions.
20. Luke 6:35.

with it were able to rejoice in being poor in spirit, mournful, and meek. It was a truth that made people hunger and thirst for righteousness, rather than believing that they were righteous because of what they believed.[21]

It seems clear from Jesus' teachings that what he sought to teach his followers was how *to be* as he was. Seventeen times throughout the Gospels, Jesus says, "Follow me." What else could he mean but *be* as I am. The truth that Jesus taught was a way to be rather than something to know and believe. It seems strange that Christians put their faith in theologies and formulas for salvation when Jesus himself never mentions such things and gives us very little from which even to form such epistemic truths. Of the one hundred and eighty three questions asked of Jesus throughout the four Gospels, he answers only three.[22] His usual response is to ask a question in return, answer a different question than one asked, or simply not answer. Furthermore, the three that he does answer have little to do with the objective nature of God or the world, but rather are about how we should respond to God and the world. The questions, "Teach us to pray," "How many times must we forgive," and "What is the greatest commandment" are questions about us and Jesus answers them because he is trying to teach his followers a divine way of being in the world.

Interestingly, although Jesus answers only three of the one hundred and eighty three questions asked of him, he asks three hundred and seven questions throughout the Gospels. How do you make theology out of that? A seminary student once asked

---

21. Matt. 5:3-6.

22. Teach us to pray. Luke 11:1; How many times must we forgive? Matt. 18:2; And, what is the greatest commandment? Matt. 22:36.

one of her professors why they never talk about Jesus in seminary but only Paul. The professor responded, "You can't make theology out of Jesus." Indeed, instead of giving us a theology or even enough from which to create a theology, Jesus offers his followers a way to *be* as he was toward God and the world. Of course, the last thing we want to do is to love our enemies and live a life of giving rather than getting. We do not want to forgive our torturers as Jesus does,[23] so we ignore the perspective and way of being that Jesus offered, and instead create a Christianity that answers our questions: namely, how do we go to heaven and avoid going to hell? That certainly sells better than the ontological truth Jesus offers, but interestingly, that question has had a great variety of answers over the years and still does.

For the early church, going to heaven was not a pressing question since most believed Jesus would be returning in their lifetime. Once a few generations had passed the question of heaven and how to get there became an issue. As the church became more established, a system of sacraments and theologies began to form, but they still did not give an answer as to who was in and who was out in terms of heaven. With the Protestant Reformation, there was a new emphasis on Scripture due to the invention of moveable type. Books had suddenly become available, and Protestants became the people of the Book. With the Reformation, there was also a new emphasis on faith, which eventually came to mean believing the right theology based upon a particular perspective and reading of the Scripture. Faith had begun as the great mystery of which Jesus spoke but, by the twentieth century, many Christians saw

---

23. Luke 23:34.

faith as a matter of being certain about the doctrines they trusted for salvation.

The way we think about the world changes over time as we have seen. For example, the ancient world understood bizarre human behavior as demonic possession. Today we explain the same behavior as psychotic disorders like schizophrenia. Literalists believe these are two phenomena rather than two different perspectives of the same thing. To believe they are different entities is to confuse the theory or perspective with the thing itself. Scientists still discuss whether light is of a wave or a corpuscular nature, but they do not believe they are talking about two different things but merely two different ways of talking about the same thing. Jesus used the vernacular and perspective of his day. No other language or perspective was available or would have been understood, but whether he cast out demons or cured schizophrenia is impossible to say. Jesus healed a person, but there is no way to know if the event and our way of talking about the event are identical. To believe that they are identical is to believe that language mirrors reality rather than simply being our way of talking about our experience. Perhaps demonic possession and schizophrenia are two different matters, and not simply two different perspectives of the same thing, but to think that they are entirely different simply because there are two different ways of talking about bizarre behavior is to confuse our perspective with the thing itself.

Of course, many people believe that words do refer to actual things, and although that is a difficult position to maintain today, it does afford those who hold such a belief a great degree of security in believing that what they know and believe represents some ultimate and absolute reality, but there are three major problems with this perspective. The first is that it is unrealistic given what we know about our history and how what we claim to know changes with our changing perspectives.

The second is that such a notion of truth is very different from the truth of which Jesus spoke. Aristotle may have convinced us that truth was something to know, but Jesus seems to insist it is something to be. Jesus' truth is not something to know but something to fall in love with because it is divinely beautiful and good, and not simply true. We do not come to know Jesus' truth by knowing and believing facts about his life, but we come to know his truth by falling in love with the things he said and did because we recognize them as divine. What we know and believe does not determine who we are. What we fall in love with determines who we are. If you believe all the right facts about Jesus' life, but do not think that loving your enemy or giving without expecting anything in return is divinely beautiful, you do not know the truth of which Jesus speaks.

The third problem with Aristotle's notion of truth as simply something to know and believe divides and separates us instead of uniting us. Trying to understand the Gospel through Aristotle's concept of truth has produced forty thousand different Christian denominations worldwide, because epistemic truth is always dependent upon a perspective that originates in someone's imagination. Jesus, however, prayed that his followers would be one,[24] and if we are ever to realize that, it will have to be because of a truth that is founded upon something more stable and enduring than human imagination and the perspectives it produces.

---

24. John 17:20-22.

Most Christians prefer a Christianity that is simply a matter of believing the right theological formulas for salvation. Such formulas sell much better than following Jesus into the kind of being to which he calls us. Furthermore, they justify their refusal to follow Jesus by claiming that He was Divine and therefore we cannot be as Jesus was. That seems to make sense, but it rests upon a notion of righteousness that is very different from that to which Jesus calls us. Many Christians think that either righteousness is a matter of right beliefs or the avoidance of what our culture tells us is sin. Jesus, however, speaks of a righteousness that comes through repentance. Not that repentance makes us righteous, but repentance opens us to the experience of God's mercy, and it is the ongoing experience of God's mercy for having failed to live as Jesus lived that eventually makes us into his merciful likeness. Those who are "forgiven little love little"[25] and, by contrast, those who realize how much mercy they have received become merciful. Interestingly, unlike epistemic truth, which separates us into thousands of denominations because of our vast variety of perspectives, the truth of our common failure to *be* as He was in terms of *Being* merciful, forgiving, and mindful of the Divine presence unites us like no theology can.

The perspectives our imagination offers to make sense of our experience do not endure for very long, and what we deem a true perspective today will no longer provide an adequate understanding tomorrow. In every generation, however, when someone forgives their torturers and shows love even toward their enemies, we recognize the Divine. This is the perennial truth,

---

25. Luke 7:47.

which does not vary with the vicissitudes of history, since it does not speak to us with words. It is a divine truth, which resonates with our *being*, if we have come to love what is truly divine. Our eternal state is determined, not by the perspective through which we claim to know what is true, but by what we recognize as beautiful and good.

Rules: Knowing them is not to living them in practice is another, not to adhere to them, but b/c you live rules, believe that is the best way to behave

Lucie Mismer — Kolodge's move out.